CIRCUIT RIDERS

FANNING THE FLAMES OF REVIVAL

Other books by Pamela Bolton:

Ushering in Revival and Awakening

God on the Move—Fanning the Flames of Revival

Lady Preachers—Fanning the Flames of Revival

Today's Glory Stories—Fanning the Flames of Revival

Circuit Riders

Fanning The Flames Of Revival

By Pamela Bolton

Circuit Riders

Fanning The Flames Of Revival

Contents

DEDICATION

This book is dedicated to all the circuit riders who went before us sharing the Gospel, while sometimes risking their lives so that people could be set free from the snares of the evil one. It is also dedicated to all the modern-day circuit riders who now travel by different modes of transportation to share the Gospel all over the world.

Foreword

Each of us has a divine destiny, to impact the world around us for the Kingdom of God! When you read Pastor Pamela Bolton's new book, *Circuit Riders—Fanning the Flames of Revival*, you will be inspired to see how much a single person can accomplish when they are fueled by passion and fully dependent on God's provision. The lives of the circuit riders were incredibly hard compared to the kind of service for Christ that most of us are accustomed to today. What an eye opening message, and what a challenge for those of us who serve in comfy churches with expensive sound systems, costly stage lights, and fresh brewed coffee every Sunday.

As you read the historical documents gathered in this book, you will get a unique perspective on the importance of the Methodist circuit rider in American frontier life. The sheer number of souls that each circuit rider helped to shepherd is staggering! Some of the anecdotes in this book are as amusing as they are educational. As a teacher and a homeschool mom, I'm also excited to make use of this valuable resource to teach a part of American History that most textbooks omit.

I hope that the next generation of leaders in American churches can get a glimpse of what their predecessors went through to spread the Gospel. They were educated by their trials and qualified by their faith. They lived and died for the glory of their Savior and endured every hardship with gladness. May we all face our unique callings with similar courage and trust the empowerment of God's Holy Spirit.

Heather Bartos, Worship Leader at Cooperstown Assembly of God, Cooperstown, NY

Introduction

THE GREAT COMMISION

And Jesus came and spake unto them, saying, "All power is given unto me in heaven and in earth.

"Go ye therefore, and teach all nations, baptizing them in the name of the Father, and of the Son, and of the Holy Ghost:

"Teaching them to observe all things whatsoever I have commanded you: and, lo, I am with you always, even unto the end of the world. Amen." Matthew 28:18-20

There is much that we can learn from the persistence, determination, and fortitude of the old circuit riders. They endured many hardships for the sake of the Gospel, and they were willing to lay down their lives, if need be, so that others could come into the saving knowledge of Jesus Christ.

There were many circuit riders from both the Methodist and Baptist Churches; however, there were some from other denominations as well, and they have left us with a rich heritage of evangelism.

Some of the more notable riders include John Wesley (Founder of Methodism, England), Frances Asbury (First Methodist Bishop in the United States), Peter Cartwright, John B. Matthias, and Wilbur Fisk. There were thousands of other circuit riders, many of whom have long since been forgotten here on this planet, but I'm sure that their names are well known in Heaven.

Today, we need more people who are willing to follow God's call on their lives, whatever it may be and wherever it may lead, whether they are ministering to two people or to 2,000 people.

In this book, we're going to take a glimpse at the lives of some of the men and women who made great sacrifices for the cause of the Gospel. We will discuss some things that we can do as the church of Jesus Christ, to position ourselves to be used by Him more effectively, to reach people in our own local neighborhoods as well as wherever else He may lead us.

We can be looking to build off of the original church foundations of 2,000 years ago as well as the testimonies of the old circuit riders, and we can be encouraged by the accounts of what took place years ago, while believing God for even GREATER things now.

As we remember what God did back then, we can allow our faith to rise; and we can be open to what He wants to do by the power of His Spirit today. He is Creator, and He is continually doing new things, which may not look like they did in past revivals and awakenings.

My prayer is that as you read, you will be encouraged, inspired, challenged, and blessed!

PLEASE NOTE: Any time that you see text in italics in Chapters 1-7, it is my writing. All other text in these chapters is directly quoted from newspaper articles, which are then cited at the end of each section of print. Some minor grammatical and spelling errors were corrected from the original newspapers, for clarity. When you see "???," this indicates places where the newspaper print is illegible.

CHAPTER 1

TYPICAL LIFE OF A CIRCUIT RIDER

In this book, I hope to honor the lives of those men and women who, under some most difficult of circumstances, ran their races and served God passionately on the mission field, especially here in the United States. No doubt, many of them are now a part of the "great cloud of witnesses" who are cheering us on from Heaven.

"**Wherefore seeing we also are compassed about with so great a cloud of witnesses, let us lay aside every weight, and the sin which doth so easily beset us, and let us run with patience the race that is set before us, Looking unto Jesus the author and finisher of our faith**; who for the joy that was set before him endured the cross, despising the shame, and is set down at the right hand of the throne of God. For consider him that endured such contradiction of sinners against himself, lest ye be wearied and faint in your minds." Hebrews 12:1-3 (KJV)

TRIBUTE TO CIRCUIT RIDERS

Rev. E. K. Hardin Says Future Historian Will Accord Them Credit

"Much of the credit that has been given to the founders of American political institutions belongs, by rights, to the circuit riders of the early days—the men who, on horseback, carried the Gospel to the remotest regions of the wilderness," asserted Rev. Edward Hardin in his sermon at Mount Vernon Place M. E. Church South yesterday. "Someday," he declared, "a historian will arise in America who will rewrite the record of the early days of the republic and give to Bishop Francis Asbury, George Whitefield, and others of the old-time circuit riders the honor that is due them in connection with the founding of the nation—'an honor,'" Rev. Hardin said, "that is richly deserved but for which those men would not care."

(Evening Star., October 19, 1914, Page 7, Image 7)

THE CIRCUIT RIDER

ITINERANT PREACHERS OF PIONEER DAYS

New Spiritual Wants of the First Settlers Were Supplies—Labors of Early Preachers—Their Miserable Pay—Hardships Endured Persons and People

Among the many peculiar characters developed in the early days of our ??? history, not the least singular was the traveling preacher, who ministered to the spiritual wants of the settlers in the backwoods. He was a natural product of the times in which he lived and of the country in which his lot was cast. He was in the most ??? sense of the word one of the people himself, for, in all probability, he had been born and reared in the immediate neighborhood of his "circuit." Nine-tenths of his auditors knew him from his boyhood, and his father and the rest of his family, and were prepared to give his pedigree back to the time when the family made its appearance in this country. Earlier than this, few knew even their own family history; and nobody cared, for it was a social principle in the early days of the colonies that nobody had a father until he came to America, and when he was here, he was as good as anybody, if not a little better.

The traveling preacher, or circuit rider, as he was generally called, was a man thoroughly and conscientiously devoted to his calling. He always believed himself to be "called" to the work of the ministry, and having this conviction, gave up everything else for its sake. His worldly belongings, barring the wife and children, that always lived somewhere within the bounds of his circuit, were generally limited to what he could carry in his saddle-bags. These usually contained a change of linen, a Bible, a hymn book, in those lays called a "hime book," and sometimes a lunch of chicken and corn bread, put up by a kindly sister at the last preaching place. He had a horse, generally a good horse, for no other kind could stand the hardships of the journeys he had to make; and for his living he trusted to Providence and the people of the various "appointments" along his route. And, as a rule, he was as well cared for as the means of the people permitted, for every family counted it an honor to have the preacher stay with them; and as he was usually the bearer of news from one neighborhood to another—he was always a welcomed guest.

Two preachers, a senior and a junior, were usually assigned to each circuit, and the appointments for the two were arranged in such a way that the people of each station had preaching every other week, at least, or sometimes every week. The labors of these self-sacrificing men were by no means, however, confined to Sunday. **They preached every day, sometimes twice a day, reaching one station at 9 or 10 in the morning, holding service, dining with some brother who lived nearby, and in the afternoon, riding on to another station, where an evening service was to be held, and repeating this round week after week, month after month, during the year until "conference" came, when the appointments were changed and the preachers went to new**

fields. Twenty or thirty sermons every four weeks were the usual work, together with 200 or 300 miles of the hardest kind of travel.

Of roads there were few, the traveler being compelled to rely on bridle paths through the forest, and often on ??? tracks aided by "blazes" on the trees or pieces of bark chopped out, having a white place underneath, which could be seen at a considerable distance and ??? aided the ??? of the wayfarer. When darkness overtook the preacher on his journey, and he could no longer discern the "blazes" on the trees, he trusted to the instinct of the horse, and when this failed, as it sometimes, though rarely, did, he was compelled to pass the night in the woods. If he had flint and steel, he made a fire, if not, he sat down at the root of a tree and held his horse until the morning.

In rainy weather, he was often compelled to swim the swollen streams that lay in his route or make long detours in search of a place where the stream could be forded. Yet all these hardships, and more, including sleeping in lofts where the snow drifted in, in rooms where four beds were placed and the family all slept in the only room in the cabin afforded, and the annoyance of having absolutely no privacy but that of the forest during this journey from one appointment to another, were cheerfully endured, and for no compensation save the consciousness of duty well done and the pittance that the people were able to give in return for the services rendered them. Money in those times was scarce, and many an old preacher has been heard to tell how in the early days of his ministry, he received but $25 or $30 from his people for a year's hard work. But this sum did not really represent all they did for him, for his entertainment was free wherever he went, and a pair of stockings here, a pair of shoes there, a wool hat or fur cap from one, a coat from another and a pair of jeans trousers from a third, eked out his scanty support very materially. Nor was this all, for on his "home round"—that is, when on that part of his circuit that brought him toward home—he might be seen with a ham or flitch of bacon on one side of his saddle, a pair of chickens or a wild turkey on the other, and, it may be a haunch of venison or a bag of corn in front, all the contributions of those who gave willingly of what they had to give at all. These, with an occasional wedding fee, a sum varying from 25c to $1, paid by a youth in his first suit of store clothes, constituted his principal reliance for a livelihood. His wife did her own work, and her neighbors brought in supplies from time to time to help out the preacher, so, on the whole, he lived about as well as they, and, what was better, was fully content with what he had, and cheerfully sang:

> "No foot of land do I possess,
> No cottage in this wilderness."

In **Kentucky, Tennessee, and the Southern States** generally, the first "meeting houses" were of logs, and in a style of architecture that closely approximated that of the settlers' cabins. Where there were schoolhouses these were used for religious purposes, but where there were none the cabins of the settlers were employed, and almost anyone, whether he was a member of the particular denomination to which the circuit rider belonged or not, was generally willing to open his house for preaching. Where regular houses were built for services, however, the neighborhood was understood to have advanced considerably on the road to refinement.

"Quarterly meeting" at one of these wayside log sanctuaries was a great occasion. The presiding elder was always there, with as many of the brethren as could be mustered. Long before the appointed hour for the service, the roads were full of primitive vehicles on the way to the meeting house. Antiquated wagons, a man and his wife on the front seat, two or three wooden chain just behind for invited guests, and the balance of the load made up of children packed in straw, were common, but more frequent were riders on horseback.

They came in twos and threes, men and women, with children in front and behind; and on arriving at the grove in which the church was situated, they tied the horses, not always far enough apart to prevent an equine dispute, scattered ear-corn on the ground in front of them to be about equally divided between the steeds and the strolling pigs that always infested the neighborhood on such occasions, and men and women separated into groups. Down at the always convenient spring, the former gathered, the elders to smoke their pipes and talk crops and their juniors to discuss politics. In and about the church, the old women talked butter and eggs or discussed the attire of the one "worldly" girl sure to be found in every neighborhood, while their daughters sat silent. For it was a favorite maxim in those days that young girls and children should be seen and not heard.

A stir in the little crowd about the door told of the arrival of the elder and his brother circuit riders, for the elder was just as much a circuit rider as the rest, except that his circuit was bigger; and a few of the nearest filed into the church, whither the preachers had preceded them. The brethren said their prayers, took their seats, conferred among themselves in loud whispers as to the order of service, and then someone struck a familiar hymn. All joined lustily, and the sound thereof, wafted out of the open windows and down the hill to the spring, notified the brethren there that "meetin' had begun," and induced an instant suspension of crop talk and a stampede in the direction of the meeting house. By the time the hymn was ended, the house was filled, and the regular service of the day began.

The preaching would hardly be acceptable in a $100,000 church nowadays, for it often happened that grammar and rhetoric were conspicuous by their absence, but there was always enthusiasm in any quantity, and also plenty of Scripture.

The old preachers of those days did not know much about the graces of oratory, but they did know all about the Bible, for it was the one book that they constantly read and that they were thoroughly conversant with from cover to cover. A proposition was started, and Bible texts in confirmation of it were cited; if it could be proved from the Bible, well and good; if not, no matter what it was, or who stated it, it was rank infidelity, and the proposer was an infidel. The nice distinctions of the higher criticism were unknown quantities; the preachers of those days knew nothing of the Javist and the Elohist. Where the apostle affirmed "Wives, submit to your husbands," they said that it meant that the women should mind, and not cherish any ideas about being equal to the man and voting. They hated gold chains and rings and silk dresses and boiled shirts and cards and fiddles and whisky, and all these things were, in their sight, almost equally abominable.

A man with spotless linen was to them a dandy; a woman with gold chains and jewelry was on the right road to perdition. Some of them preached against these things and denounced unsparingly all who favored them. Cards and fiddles were there pet aversion, and when, as sometimes happened, a mischievous person went to a "protracted meeting" or a camp meeting with a fiddle, jug of whisky, and/or pack of cards, the preachers were sometimes known to knock down and drag out the offender with as much energy as would be shown by any shoulder-hitting son of Belial in the country.

Their meetings did not lack for vivacity from other causes. In those days, no man stirred abroad without his gun and his dog, and a concourse of people was the occasion also for a concourse of dogs. Generally, curs of low degree, they had neither patience nor pedigree, and dog fights at meetings were matters of by no means infrequent occurrence. When they took place outside, the curs were generally left to settle their dispute among themselves, unless it became too noisy. But when this occurred, some man seated near the door and armed with a good-sized whip, quietly slipped out to act as umpire, and a moment later a series of yelps, followed by silence, gave indication that the war was over. More of an incident was when they when they took place within the limits of the congregation, for every other exercise was at once suspended until the belligerents could be parted.

When the church had a floor raised a few feet from the ground, the space beneath was not infrequently used by vagrant swine as a place of temporary abode; and when, as sometimes happened, the dogs took into their heads the notion that the hogs were trespassers and ought to be evicted, the trouble was more serious from the difficulty of reaching the battlefield, a difficulty that was finally surmounted by sending in a boy with a cowhide to eject both dogs and pigs.

Such trifles as crying babies were never noticed in a congregation of this kind; crying was popularly supposed to be good for the lungs of the infant, and the mother let it cry, with such efforts to soothe it as occurred to her on the spur of the moment, or were suggested by interested friends.

To the people of the present time with their $500,000 churches and $6,000 preachers, with organ and choir and Sunday-school appointments of the most elegant description, such services seem farcical and lacking in proper reverence. But it should not be forgotten that all these things are merely comparative, and that to the people of the latter part of the eighteenth and early years of the nineteenth century, the religious elegances of the present would have seemed just as inappropriate. The preachers and the singing were to their taste. To them the eloquence of a Talmage and the music of a Handel would have been only words and noise. They could understand their preacher, and could sing their "himes," and were satisfied with both. To them, separate hymn books would have been a superfluity, for many of them could not read, and one hymn book, held by the preacher, who "lined" the hymn, that is, gave out two lines of the hymn at a time for the people to sing, was enough for the whole congregation.

The old preachers have mostly passed away, but the results of their works are seen in the thousands of churches that everywhere dot the country districts, many of them on the identical spots where the log cabins once stood that were sanctified by the presence and labors of the early circuit riders. And the system still continues, and some readers may be surprised to learn that many thousands of country people in the North, West, and South have now no other religious services than those conducted by the circuit riders. The times have changed for these too, and now they wear broadcloth and ride in buggies instead of on horseback, to their appointments. Their churches are of boards, or even of brick, and have choirs and cabinet organs, and the women wear feathers in their hats and the men polish their boots, and the girls have earrings and finger rings and beaux, but the principles are the same, and the system is almost identical with that known to our grandfathers.

(The Globe-Republican., February 01, 1895, Image 2)

PRAISES WORK OF ITINERANT CIRCUIT RIDER

College Professor Gives Estimate of Character of Early Middle-West Preachers

Madison, WI, April 14 (*1921*)—The work of the circuit riders, those hardy characters who a century ago were scouring with the Gospel the freshly opening middle west, was appraised today by the historian at the Mississippi Valley Historical Association meeting here.

Prof. W. M. Gewehr of Morningside College told the association that the needs of the frontier religion of the period were best met by itinerant system of the early western Methodism, and that the success of the itineracy depended above all on the activities of that zealous and devoted army of circuit riders, who braved every peril, hardship, suffering and privation incident to frontier life."

On every highway, Professor Gewehr said that the circuit riders became familiar figures with their straight-breasted coats, short breeches and long stockings, the oil-skin covering for the hat, the leather saddle bags, and the hair clipped short in front and allowed to hang down the back of the head to the shoulders.

"Such was their faithfulness," Professor Gewehr said, "in filling their appointment that on days that were so bitterly cold as to drive most persons indoors it was a proverbial saying, **'There is nothing out today but crows and Methodist preachers.'"**

The circuits were large, often four or five hundred miles in circumference and required from three to six weeks to travel. They swept over the whole country, touching at neighborhoods that were very remote and distant from one another.

"In the course of a four weeks' circuit, the itinerant would meet from twenty-five to thirty-five appointments and preach on an average of once a day. The number of preaching places was constantly being increased as new societies were collected, and circuits had to be divided.

All Turned Out

"His coming was the occasion of a general turn out of the Methodist families, and the itinerant was always sure of a congregation when he reached his appointment.

"To enter the itinerancy, as is well known, was almost equivalent to taking the vows of poverty, chastity and obedience. From 1800 to 1816, the salary of a traveling preacher was placed at $80 a year and traveling expenses, with the same allowance for a wife and $16 for each child from 7 to 14 years.

"Small as the amount was, the preacher was fortunate if he could collect half of his own allowance while on provision for the family the discipline was a perfect dead letter. Often the preachers did not get enough in a year to buy a suit of clothes or an overcoat, while it was a most serious misfortune to have to buy a new horse. Had it not been for the fact that now and then the circuit riders were presented with homespun clothing, many a preacher would have been forced to abandon the itinerancy in order to earn enough to clothe himself.

"As it was, their clothes were often but patch on patch so that the original cloth could scarcely be detected. In 1896, when Ashbury was at the Western Conference, he found the brethren 'in want and could not suit (clothe) themselves; so, I parted with my watch, my coat, and my shirt.' Notwithstanding their abject poverty, these men were never too poor to deny themselves for someone who might be worse off. Their lives were indeed examples of the Spirit of Christ.

"The poverty of the itinerancy made it almost out of the question for the circuit rider to marry and establish a family."
(The Rock Island Argus., April 15, 1921)

EARLY CITY HISTORY

Contributions on the Early Days of Richmond Will Appear in This Column Daily

THE CIRCUIT RIDERS

The best account of these noble and courageous men, I have found in Eggleston's story of "The Circuit Rider." **It depicts in glowing language their zeal, self-denial, and perseverance**—the danger and hardship they endured to stem the tide of lawlessness. On the frontier was a class of men who were murderers, horse thieves, and gamblers; having no permanent homes but raiding the whole country; to the terror of the honest settlers.

The first circuit formed in Indiana was in 1807 and was called the Whitewater Circuit. Rev. Joseph Williams was the preacher in charge. The circuit embraced all of **Indiana**. In 1808, he reported that there were but 160 members of the First Methodist Church within his circuit. **In one year, these circuit riders would cover 5,000 miles, filling from 500 to 600 appointments and having the care of numberless scattered churches in the wilderness. These preachers endured many hardships.** There were no roads except "blazed" bridle paths, through much of the country. The streams were unbridged, and they traveled with their guns on their shoulders to defend themselves from man and beast. In the very early times, there were no church buildings to accommodate the congregation, and it was literally true that **"The Groves were God's first temples."** In one of these groves, the first Methodist Camp Meeting was held in **Wayne County, IN,** in the fall of 1810. They would generally last a week and would be attended by hundreds, many of whom rode from fifteen to twenty miles on horseback. These preachers seldom received any salary, consequently they dressed in the plainest homespun that was contributed by some of their parishioners. Some even travelled barefoot without hat or change of clothing.

It was said of Russell Biglow that his clothes were ill-fitting blue drilling. He was unshaven and his long hair reached his shoulders. Yet, in spite of his appearance, his denunciation of sin has such an effect on his congregation that many were seized with that curious nervous affection called the "jerks," and were not able to walk or keep their hats on. Methodism was introduced into **Richmond, IN,** in 1822. He preached in a small log schoolhouse and organized a class of seven members, with George Smith as leader. These preachers referred everything to God in prayer, and the belief in divine direction was often carried to a ludicrous extent. Various devices were invented for obtaining divine direction. **Lorenzo Dow, an eccentric minister, used to suffer his horse to take his own course when he reached the forks in a road, feeling sure there was work for him in that direction.**

Others would open the Bible at random, and the first text that arrested their attention was an indication of divine leading. These texts frequently formed the subject of their discourse. They played upon the fears of their audience by such remarks as the following: "You are hair-hung and breeze-shaken over hell."

"You don't say," remarked a scoffer on the edge of the crowd. Again, he remonstrated: "You'll go to hell, and when you get there, your ribs will be nothing but a gridiron to roast your soul in."

"Hurrah for the gridiron," cried the unappalled scoffer.
MRS. SARAH A. WRIGLEY
(The Richmond Palladium and Sun Telegram., February 10, 1916)

HOLY, "KNOCK-'EM-DOWN" PREACHERS[1]

BOILING HOT RELIGION

Early Methodist sermons emphasized the practical, the immediate, and the dramatic. **"People love the preacher who makes them feel," observed Methodist preacher Thomas Ware.** The typical circuit rider preached from a basic set of Scripture texts embellished with anecdotes and analogies from everyday life. The few expository skills he used were largely gleaned from the sermons of colleagues. But **he also learned to preach with what the itinerant Henry Smith referred to as an irresistible "holy, 'knock-'em-down' power."**

Nothing would have been more anathema to Methodist itinerants than the dispassionate reading of a prepared sermon. They preached extemporaneously, without notes or manuscript. As Bishop Asbury once urged one of his preachers, "Feel for the power; feel for the power, Brother."

GRUELING PACE

The early circuit riders preached and traveled at a grueling pace. John Brooks, for example, labored so intensely during his first three years in the itinerancy that he reported, "I lost my health and broke a noble constitution." During one tempestuous revival, Brooks lay "sick in bed," but he said, "the people literally forced me out, and made me preach."

In 1799, itinerant Billy Hibbard rode the **Cambridge, NY**, circuit, **a 500-mile, four-week circuit with up to 63 preaching appointments**, in addition to the responsibility of meeting the classes. **In one year on the Flanders, NJ, circuit, Thomas Smith estimated he traveled 4,200 miles, preached 324 times, exhorted 64 times, and met classes 287 times.**

Indeed, in many parts of the new nation, Methodist preachers suddenly seemed to be everywhere, leading one New Yorker to exclaim in 1788, "I know not from whence they all come, unless from the clouds."

Circuit riders also frequently had to contend with poor or uncertain lodging. Most often the itinerants stayed with sympathetic families along their routes, though they sometimes lodged at inns or slept in the open.

At the end of one weary day in the **North Carolina** back country, the itinerant, Thomas Ware, sought shelter at the isolated cabin of a young couple.

"The man gave me to understand, at once, that I could not stay there," recounted Ware. "I looked at him, and smiling, said, 'that would depend upon our comparative strength.'" Unwilling to wrestle the Methodist preacher, the couple relented—and in the morning, Ware baptized their children.

Bishop Francis Asbury set the standard for all early Methodist itinerants and left little doubt as to what he expected from his charges. **He visited nearly every state once a year. One biographer estimates that Asbury stayed in 10,000 households and preached 17,000 sermons.**

CHAPTER 2

CIRCUIT RIDER TRIVIA AND TIDBITS

POEM

WHEN THE CIRCUIT RIDER CAME

In the backwoods of Ohio, in the days of long ago,
When religion was religion, not a dressy fashion show,
When the spirit of the Master fell as flames of living fire.
And the people did the singing, not a trained artistic choir,
There was scarcely seen a ripple in life's gently flowing tide,
No events to draw the people from their daily toil aside,
Naught to set the pious spirit of the pioneers aflame,
Save upon the rare occasions when the circuit rider came.

He was usually mounted on the sorriest of nags,
All his outfit for the journey packed in leather saddle bags,
And he'd travel with the Bible or the hymn book in his hand
Reading sacred words or singing of the happy Promised Land,
How the toiling wives would glory in the dinners they would
spread,
And how many a hapless chicken or a turkey lost its head
By the gleaming chopper wielded by the hand of a sturdy dame.
For it wasn't very often that the circuit rider came.

All the settlement around us, would be ringing with the news
That there'd be a meetin' Sunday, and we'd "taller" up our
shoes,
And we'd brush our homespun dress suits, pride of every
country youth.

And we'd grease our hair with marrow till it shone like golden truth.
And the frocks of Linsey-Woolsey would be donned by all the girls.
And with heated old fire pokers, they would make their corkscrew curls;
They were scarcely queens of fashion, but were lovely just the same.
And they always looked their sweetest when the circuit rider came.

As a preacher, holy Moses! How he'd swing the living Word,
How he'd draw the pious "bretherin'" yet closer to the Lord,
And he'd raise the hair of sinners sitting on the back-most seat,
With his fiery, lurid pictures of the everlasting heat!
We have sat in grand cathedrals, triumphs of the builder's skill,
And in great palatial churches 'neath the organ's mellow thrill,
But they never roused within us such a reverential flame,
As would burn in that old schoolhouse when the circuit rider came.

JAMES BARTON ADAMS in *Denver Post*
(The Dupuyer Acantha., November 01, 1900, Image 6)

EARLY STATE CHURCHES

The early churches in **Indiana** were first held in homes. When more people came into the neighborhood, they held their services in a schoolhouse. Then, the people built churches, and the ground around them was used for a cemetery.

These churches were heated by fireplaces and sometimes by pots of red-hot coals, which the people would bring. (*Doesn't this sound like real commitment? *For a believer, attending church was something to be taken seriously.*)

* "Not forsaking the assembling of ourselves together, as the manner of some is; but exhorting one another: and so much the more, as ye see the day approaching." Hebrews 10:25 (KJV)

———————

There were traveling preachers called circuit riders, and when they were in the woods, they would follow a blazed trail. The blazed trail was made by notching trees.
MAURICE MENTENIDCK—5 B Hibberd School
(The Richmond Palladium and Sun-telegram., December 16, 1916, HOME EDITION, THE JUNIOR PALLADIUM, Page 6, Image 18)

———————

The Bowling Green Post (**Bowling Green, MO**) quotes the poultry market in that town as follows: Plain Baptist chickens sell for 25 cents per head. Fair to medium Methodist chickens, suitable for circuit riders or local preachers, bring 30 cents, while extra-fine yellow legs, good enough for presiding elders, come as high as 35 cents. On Presbyterian roosters, prices fluctuate according to propinquity or remoteness of the synod or presbytery. Other denominations rate up or down, owing to the urgency of the demand.
(Monroe City Democrat., December 11, 1902, CHRISTMAS NUMBER, Image 16)

———————

The following is an excerpt from "The Circuit Riders," contributed by Bishop Hamilton to *The Youth Companion*. It *speaks* of early times in the West, and standing prominently out is the contrast between the unselfish devotion of good men then and the lucre scooping… and lesser evangelical lights of today.

Into those conditions of life came an order of itinerant preachers and teachers, like the prophets of old, to meet the exigencies of the times. President William Henry Harrison, in describing the "circuit rider," wrote thus: "They are men whom no labor tires, no scenes disgust, no danger frightens, in the discharge of their duty. To gain recruits for their Master's service, they sedulously seek out the victims of vice in the abodes of misery and wretchedness. The vow of poverty is not taken by these men, but their conduct is precisely such as it would have been had they taken one; their stipulated pay is barely signed them. With much the larger portion, the horse, which they can call their own, and the contents of their valise or saddlebags are the sum total of their earthly possessions."

(The Richmond Palladium and Sun-telegram., August 18, 1909, Image 1)

THE WONDERFUL GROWTH OF METHODISM

...For 100 years, Methodism has been a great evangelical force. In the early days, the circuit riders carried the Gospel of Christ to the remotest settlements. **Brave and hardy men were they, zealous in the Master's service, spreading his Word to rich and poor alike, careless of personal discomfort, thinking only of the saving of souls. They planted churches wherever they could get a few faithful souls together and laid broad and deep foundations of a great national and international church.** They have gone abroad to the uttermost parts of the earth, and carried Christianity to many strange lands, and preached in many foreign tongues. The church of America has grown rich and powerful in the last 100 years and is able to raise vast sums of money to carry on its work throughout the world. **The seed planted by that little, despised, and ridiculed band of religious enthusiasts in Oxford College so many years ago has developed a mighty force to sway the world for good.**

(The Ocala Banner., August 22, 1919, Page 8, Image 12)

TOO MUCH VELVET

Good salaries, well-appointed studies, and soft bottomed chairs seem to have played havoc with that hardy spirit of endurance which once characterized the country parson in this neck of the woods.

The days when the preacher slept on his horse, carried his sermons in his head, his Bible in his pocket, and a clean shirt in his saddlebags have gone glimmering.

When **Peter Cartwright** was shouting the Gospel across the prairies and over the hills of **Southern Illinois**, half a century ago, he never stopped to inquire whether the roads were good or whether there was a bed and a beefsteak at the other end of the line. He simply laid the lash on his nag (*horse*) and sailed away, one mile or fifty, and trusted to Providence for food and a congregation. **If there was no "meetin' house," he chose a stump; and if there was no stump, he stood on the ground; and if his audience was not respectful, he thumped it into submission with his bare knuckles.**

Old Peter had no salary, no study, and no soft-bottomed chairs—no organist, no choir leader, no thousand-dollar soprano, no beautiful white tie, and no $40 Prince Albert; and he was no D.D., but he was right there with the goods in a religious way, and he had made the whole of the middle West thoroughly acquainted with the doctrine of the strenuous life long before Theodore Roosevelt was ever heard or thought of.

Now, what is this we hear? **A Missouri preacher has been relieved of a portion of his pastorate at his own request because he considered it too much of a hardship to ride nine miles to a certain point Sunday afternoon, conduct services, and then return to the starting point in time for evening services there.**

Oh, very well! But what would the old-fashioned circuit riders say, were they here, to the soft muscled young (*men*) who shy at so easy a stunt as that? Are pipe organs and velvet cushions enervating (*causing them to be tired*)?

POST DISPATCH

(Monroe City Democrat., May 07, 1903, Image 7)

PREACHER PAID IN EGGS

Circuit Rider's Story Told at M. E. Conference, St. Louis

The hardships of a Methodist circuit rider were brought forcibly to the attention of the city ministers attending the St. Louis conference of the Methodist Episcopal Church when one country preacher reported that in the last two months he had received half of a hog and a great many eggs, but no money. He had sent twelve dozen eggs to the District Superintendent, he said. Another circuit rider said he had received $19 in two months, and a third that he had received no money, but that his parishioners had promised to buy him a horse before winter and had entertained him liberally in their homes.

(The Nassau Post., November 05, 1915, Page 2)

TOO HOT FOR HIM

Pastor Quit Because Booze Running Roads Unsafe

Rev. Frank H. Wright, pastor of the Wesleyan Methodist church at **West Chazy**, near **Plattsburg, NY**, was obliged to give up his pastorate and become a professor in Houghton Seminary on account of the excitement attendant upon "booze running," he told the church conference in session here. He said he had two charges and was obliged to cover 40 miles in three-night trips each week. Even with a rifle in the car and driving in the ditch, he said he made up his mind the roads of Northern New York were unsafe for ministerial circuit riders and gave up his charge.

PHILADELPHIA RECORDER
(The Whitesville News., September 07, 1922, Page 7, Image 7)

TALES OF THE OLD FRONTIER

CIRCUIT RIDER DAYS AND WAYS

...The circuit riders preached in a day of rough living, and more than once, they were called upon to use physical strength in turning the particularly ungodly from the path of sin. Once a band of rowdies interrupted the meeting that was being conducted by one of these churchmen militant. He did not hesitate for a second. Springing over the pulpit of the rude little log cabin church, he strode down the aisle, seized two or three of the disturbers, and threw them to the floor. Then he sat on them, and as be bumped their heads together repeatedly, he remarked: "Well, boys, if I can't beat religion into you, I'll beat the devil out of you."

And he did it so thoroughly that they never again disturbed his meetings.

This doesn't sound very politically correct to me.
(Chateaugay Record and Franklin County Democrat., December 14, 1923, Page 12)

"THE SAWDUST TRAIL"

The "Sawdust Trail," James J. Jeffries, the former heavyweight champion, we learn is about to "hit the sawdust trail," in that he intends to lead others along. That is to say, Mr. Jeffries proposes to become an evangelist and will enter upon his new work this spring.

It could hardly be believed that the slaughter-breathing Saul of Tarsus would become the foremost of apostles and at last suffer the martyrdom which he had imposed upon others. Virile men since then have been led from lives of violence into peaceful work for Christianity. **Peter Cartwright, the most powerful of the circuit riders who spread Methodism throughout the west the first years of the last century, cut short a disordered youth to enter the ministry and became for a half century a presiding elder. He blazed the way for the church through the wilderness of Kentucky and Tennessee to Illinois, and all the time with tongue or fist overcame the foes of righteousness**.

But we cannot believe that one of them, whether sincere or not, has failed to accomplish some good and has not made some appeal which has brought men to the better way.

The old circuit riders excited the emotions of their hearers, just as the sensational revivalists of today excite emotions and produce an exaltation of spirit, which in many of the hearers soon passes but lingers with others as a fixed belief in religion. There are many such believers who could never have been reached by conventional preaching. In our cities today with their multiplicity of churches, there are thousands of people who are as isolated from religious influence as the mountaineers of **Kentucky** and **Tennessee** and the frontiersmen of **Ohio, Indiana,** and **Illinois** would have been but for the coming of the circuit riders.

To such dwellers in our cities and towns come such heralds of the Gospel as Sam Jones, Billy Sunday, and now Jeffries.

(Arizona Republican., March 06, 1922, Page 4, Image 4)

HOLY, "KNOCK-'EM-DOWN" PREACHERS[1]

BAPTIZING COMMON PLACES

American Methodists soon redefined sacred space. By 1785, only 60 Methodist chapels had been purchased or built, but there were more than 800 recognized preaching places. Meetings were held in homes (where the majority of weekday sermons were delivered), courthouses, schoolhouses, the meeting houses of other denominations, barns, or in the open.

While riding the St. Lawrence Circuit in 1813, Benjamin Paddock regularly preached in a dry goods store in **Potsdam, New York**. Likewise, **Robert R. Roberts once preached in a tavern in northwestern Pennsylvania, though not without difficulty. Partway through Roberts's discourse, a drunkard in the audience awoke, calling out, "Landlord, give me a grog!" When Roberts protested granting the man's request, the tavern owner replied, "Mr. Roberts, you appear to be doing well; I would thank you to mind your own business, and I will mine."**

BISHOPS OF THE WILDERNESS

When the late Archbishop Robert Machray (*Anglican*), primate of all **Canada**, became bishop of Rupert's Land in 1865, he "had a diocese nearly as large as the whole of Europe, but without a mile of railroad in it or a steamboat." **He was missionary to a population consisting of roving Indians and white traders and trappers**, says *The Youth's Companion*.

The "bishop's court" was a log house, his coach—a dog sledge or a bark canoe, his food—pemmican (*mixture of fat and protein*) and dried fish. The man was a fellow and master of arts of Cambridge University. He went to his wild charge nearly 40 years ago, and living unmarried and alone, devoted himself wholly to the service of those whose spiritual welfare had been placed in his keeping. He was both a noble individual and a type. The work he did in Rupert's Land others did before him in the wilderness of **Canada** and the great west. Still others are carrying it on after him—men not only of his own church but of others. Of the same class were the French missionaries who first carried the Word of God to the Indians of the **Great Lakes and the Mississippi**; and to the same noble order belonged Marcus Whitman, of **Oregon**, and Bishop Whipple and Bishop Taylor and the men who have made the religious history of **Alaska**, and **the old circuit riders whose church was the woods and whose pulpit was a stump**. Wherever other men—the hunter, the trapper, the gold seeker, and the farmer—have gone for gain, these men have gone for love of God and the joy of serving Him. **Their lives make a chapter of history as inspiring as the Acts of those Apostles who first went out into the world to preach the Gospel.**

(The St. Lawrence Herald., July 22, 1904, Page 1, Image 1)

LITTLE LESSON ON MANNERS

Circuit Rider Knew His Hearers and Addressed Them in Words That They Understood

There lingers yet in the caverns of memory the concinnity of a circuit rider in the West Virginia mountains who held forth one night in an old schoolhouse on the high peak of Big Sewell. The building was of unhewn logs, with press-pole roof and puncheon floor, the men seated on one side, the women on the other. The aged preacher arose and addressed his congregation somewhat as follows.

"Now, brethren and sisters, before I begin the services of the night, I will give you some advice on elegance of manners. You all wear store boots, and the women wear brogans. Now, in moving your feet on this puncheon floor it makes a loud bumping and ugly noise if you scrape your boots along, which perturbs everybody. So don't drag your feet; lift them up straight and set them down soft, and do not drag them across the floor. Cough, spit, hawk, or sneeze as little as you can; and if a man has to go out to see if his horse is tied, to blow his nose, or to go to the spring, or for any other reason, step light on the floor in them cowhide boots and brogans. We will now sing the twenty-third hymn."

The good old preacher, when he referred to persons going out for some undesignated purpose, probably knew that the backsliders present had a jug near the spring.

(Hickory Daily Record., February 14, 1916, Page 4, Image 4)

A NEW STYLE OF CONVERTING SINNERS

To Build a Church on Wheels and Drive It Through the Country with Four Horses

CLYDE, NY

May 22—Mr. Osborn, the drummer evangelist, who has been holding revivals here, has devised a new plan of introducing the Gospel. **The idea of Mr. Osborn is to reach as many as possible of the class of people who do not attend church. He will build a large chariot and make a pilgrimage through the country. This church on wheels will be large enough to hold a company of sinners and a piano, and will furnish a** place from which the evangelist can address his audiences. It will go from town to town drawn by four horses. The drummer evangelist will receive financial backing from Mr. Sheldon, a wealthy resident of Auburn.

(The Portland Daily Press., May 23, 1895, Image 1)

CHAPTER 3

CIRCUIT RIDERS' STORIES

IN THEIR OWN WORDS

"We must reach every section of America, especially the raw frontiers. We must not be afraid of men, devils, wild animals, or disease. Our motto must always be FORWARD!"— Francis Asbury (1745-1816)—*one of the first bishops of the Methodist Church in the United States.*

This is what our motto should be as well.

THE CIRCUIT RIDER

"There is no period in my ministerial life, and I have seen sixty-one years in the service, that rejoices my recollection as does that period of itinerary, during my first years in the work, when I sat in the saddle of the circuit rider," said Rev. James Erwin, D.D., recently.

"Our ministers of today would be ill-fitted to endure the fatigue and hardships we were called upon to endure in those days," said he. "Our circuits were often four hundred and five hundred miles long, and it took us a month to get around the circuit, preaching a sermon every day in the year and three sermons on Sunday. Our sermons were greatest and broadest when measured lengthwise. Our plan for the circuit called for thirty-eight sermons, and this, of course, necessitated much repetition. News traveled slowly in those days, and we were not afraid of criticism. Sometimes, three sermons were the only stock taken for a whole month's journey, but they were added unto at every place and modified and made better as we went along. We had a wonderful faculty of selecting texts for our sermons. The same sermon was preached from many texts. A sermon could be improved by repetition. We were continually in the saddle from one month's end to the other, except when we stopped to refresh ourselves or to preach. We were always cordially received everywhere, and the best in the house, and that was such as we would call rather plain fare now, was placed at our disposal. We would call at one place in the morning, eat a hearty meal, preach a sermon, hold a class meeting in the evening, catch what sleep we could, and start on our way again as early as possible in the morning. No matter what the weather, we had to make our circuit, for the people depended on us and would gather at the stopping place from miles around to await our coming and get the news. The circuit rider was the most speedy and reliable mail service of the day. Upon our plan or schedule were the names of places and people with whom we were expected to stop, and at those houses, usually log cabins, we were expected to preach. Here the people gathered and waited for us. Our sermons were usually an hour and a half or two hours long, but those who came to hear us never tired of them, though the sermons, especially if we had repeated them a good many times, sometimes tired us.

"Many times, we did not stop at the places put upon the schedule because of special invitation, but we always went to the house allotted to us to preach and to see if there were any notices left there for weddings or funerals. Sometimes bridal couples would meet us at the house and would be married there, though such were exceptional instances. If there was a notice of a funeral, we were expected to leave our circuit and cut across the country to the house, sometimes thirty miles or so, to perform the burial rite, leaving the station to be supplied by some local preacher. Though people could time their marriages so that we could serve them, people could not so time their deaths. We had to go to the graves from great distances, through rain and snow, through mud and rivers, that those whose friends desired them to have a Christian burial might do so.

"After the burial, we would again mount and get back to our circuit as soon as possible. Although our hardships were not few, we usually enjoyed ourselves; and we had many blessed meetings on our way. We were sometimes overtaken in a snowsquall or a rainstorm, or we stopped by a river which had overflowed its banks. But I was never delayed in my travels, though many were. I was always fortunate enough to get some farmer to ferry me over the stream, and then I would get a horse on the other side and go on. One night, I was overtaken in a great storm and had to stay out in the woods all night. Hundreds of times, I have been so chilled through that I have had to be lifted from my horse. Then I would get a good rubbing, a warm meal, and would preach one of the best sermons of my life. I can never speak of those times without becoming awakened and feeling a new life within me.

"A wonderful affection usually sprang up between the circuit rider and his horse. Many times, I have started out with only twenty-five cents in my pocket and no place on my plan where I could stop and get anything to eat. In those cases, I would stop at some inn and let my horse have something to eat, while I went all day long fasting. Sometimes we would come to a mire in the road in the woods, and the horse would get stuck. Then we would have to dismount, get a rail or stick of some kind, and pry him out. If we knew that we were coming to a mire, we would dismount and let the horse get across alone, and then make our way to the other side as best we could. At our stations, we gave our horses the best care we could, though we sometimes were obliged to let them stand in a woodshed. Then one neighbor would bring in a bundle of hay, another would fetch a few ears of corn, and another would supply something else. We circuit riders were clothed in much the same way our

horses were fed. If our clothing became seedy, we would get a pair of pantaloons in one place, a vest at the next station, and a coat further on. Our pay was always in 'store pay.' It was very seldom that we saw a bit of money. A married circuit rider usually had what was called a 'rest week.' That means that he could stay with his family three days out of the month. The rest of the month, he was on the road and would not see his family again until he had completed his circuit. I have slept many times with two or three inches of snow on my bed."
SYRACUSE STANDARD
   (The Wichita Daily Eagle., December 23, 1892, Page 6, Image 6)

PIONEER CIRCUIT RIDER TELLS
OF EARLY DAYS

It all happened so long ago; there is only one man living to tell about it. The Methodists held a revival in the frame courthouse building which adorned a site near the end now occupied by Tarrant's massive granite structure One convert was made at this revival, and this convert was the first in Fort Worth for many a year. The hopeful, traveling revivalists, assisted by circuit riders, had long prayed for a convert. They had struggled with the rough culture of the primitive but sturdy inhabitants, and the first breach in the crust of unbelief was the signal for a flood of other converts. It happened early in 1873.

Following this revival, a crowd of cowboys gathered in a tavern just opposite the courthouse and held forth in jubilee. One of the boys pretended to be a preacher, and there was shouting and singing throughout the entire night. When asked by "the law" to close this meeting, the adherents steadfastly refused, stating that they were holding a revival of their own.

With much good-natured but deep-rooted opposition to the spread of religion in **Fort Worth**, **TX**, in those early days, the Methodist circuit rider had to be a man of courage and determination. He was also subjected to the perils of Indian raids.

Rev. J. P. Musset, 72, of Polytechnic, did most of the preaching at this revival. He can remember the time when circuit riders reported their horses stolen by Indians and especially mentions a case where one of the preachers reported such a loss at a conference, and the conference took appropriate money to furnish the rider with a new horse.

"Salary!" echoed Rev. Mr. Mussett, when asked what the pay of the early preacher amounted to. "For the first year I preached in a circuit, I received $34.75. I was 20 years old then."

Speaking of the Central Methodist Conference to be held Nov. 15 in the church where the first one met in **Waxahachie** fifty years ago, Rev. Mr. Mussett said he is the only minister surviving who was in full connection with the conference of fifty years ago at the time it convened. This conference was called the Northwest Texas Conference, but when the Central Texas Conference was formed, it kept the archives of the old Northwest Conference, and therefore considers its first meeting to have been held in 1866.

"In 1865, James N. Johnson, a circuit rider, tied his horse along **Mary's Creek in Mason County** to leave him standing for a while in order to preach. While he was preaching, the Indians stole the horse."

"At the conference in 1873, I was put on a circuit in **Johnson County** with twenty appointments and some in **Parker County. Sundays, I would preach three times. I would tie my horse to a tree near the place where the meeting was being held and kneel beside him, and pray that**

the Indians did not steal him while the meeting was going on."—*Fort Worth Star Telegram*
(Waxahachie Daily Light., November 14, 1916)

THE CIRCUIT RIDER

"The Methodist preacher of today, standing in his costly broadcloth in a fine church, preaching to a large and well-dressed congregation, is a far different personage from the Methodist circuit riders of forty years ago," said Rev. C. G. Trusdell, presiding elder of the Chicago district, as he leaned back in his comfortable armchair and fell into a reminiscent strain of thought, to a *Chicago Evening News* reporter.

"When I look back to the old days," continued the divine, "and recall the incidents that befell me when, as a young man, I was a circuit rider, it seems as if they were terribly hard times. Yet, when I was a circuit rider, I did not much mind it; and I suppose I endured as many hardships as the average circuit rider. Looking back to those days, they seem strange enough; and a listener hearing of the trials of a circuit rider would naturally say that his was a hard lot. Well, perhaps it was, but after all they were fulfilling their duty; and their aim was a higher one than many who have easier times."

"A circuit rider was distinguished from a stationed preacher by having two or more appointments to fill, whereas the regular preacher was stationed at some place where there is a congregation sufficiently large to require all his time and energies in looking after it. But a circuit rider was a Methodist preacher who, taking the Word of God under his arm, would mount his trusty steed and ride from place to place in his circuit, preaching to the farmers who gathered to hear him. My first circuit was in **Iowa**, and I was obliged to travel through **Tama, Marshall, and Story Counties**. I had from six to ten appointments, and you may rest assured I was kept busy. Every

Sunday in the year, I preached three times—morning, afternoon, and evening—and ofttimes during the week. I would get up early Sunday morning and, after eating my breakfast and seeing that my horse was properly cared for, start off for my first appointment, ten or fifteen miles away. I carried my Bible with me and went merrily along over the country roads, singing to myself and exchanging salutations with the few people I met on the road. When I arrived at my first appointment, which was about ten o'clock, 1 would generally hold services and then take my dinner at some farmer's house. And oh, how the people would turn out on those occasions! I tell you, they didn't have a chance to go to church every day in the week, nor every Sunday; and when a preacher did come along, no matter how bad the weather was, they turned out to the man and gave him a rousing welcome that half did away with the discomforts of one's long journey."

"After a good substantial dinner at some farmer's house, I would set out again and ride to my next place. 1 would preach there in the afternoon and then ride to the next place and preach there that night. Then, I'd stay all night at some farmer's and the next morning continue on my circuit. The people always used me well—I believe they always did use circuit riders well; and wherever I stopped, I was always sure of getting the best the house could afford. It was those little things that made me forget the hard and disagreeable part of my work. For it was hard and disagreeable; there is no use in denying that. I would like to see some of the ministers of today riding over all kinds of roads, in all kinds of weather, traveling through rain, snow, and sleet, perhaps with garments soaked or frozen, swimming creeks and putting up with hard fare, preaching in a miserable little school-house, or in the open air, or in some farmer's dwelling."

"A circuit rider didn't draw a princely salary, either. The first year I was a circuit rider, I didn't get a cent of pay—saw only twenty-five cents during the entire time. But then I didn't mind that. There were hundreds more circuit riders not a bit better off than myself; very few got $100 a year. **Ready money was a scarce article in those days, but the lack of it never stopped a circuit rider from fulfilling his duties. Oh, I could go ahead and talk all night about my experience as a circuit rider, but there is no use in it. Why, I remember one day during a rainy spell, I tried to urge my horse to swim across a creek that was swollen by recent rains, but the horse couldn't make it; and I narrowly escaped with my life. But the farmer's boys where I was going dragged me out, loaned me dry clothes, and I went on my way rejoicing.** That was but one of many incidents that served to make up my life as a circuit rider."

(Daily Independent., January 05, 1891, Image 4)

"While riding through the rain and dark, with no human being with me, my soul was comforted on the reflection of the omnipresence of my Saviour: I felt He was near to bless and preserve me,....."—Isaac Boring, 1829

"Thanks be to God! He compensated me for all my toil; for many precious souls were awakened and converted to God."—Freeborn Garrettson

CHAPTER 4

THE CIRCUIT RIDER

CHANGING MODES OF TRANSPORTATION

NEWS-DISPATCH, UNION, N. Y., JANUARY 1, 1920

Modern Circuit Rider Uses Flivver
"THE KING'S BUSINESS REQUIRES HASTE"

(What is a Flivver? A cheap car or plane, a clunker)

CIRCUIT RIDING—OLD AND NEW

The twentieth century circuit rider who has congregations scattered over from ten to fifty square miles of territory does not travel from place to place on horseback. Instead, he makes use of two of the latest methods of transportation, immeasurably faster than the slow-paced

Dobbin. He either mounts a motorcycle and pfut-pfuts his way from one village to another or climbs into a moderate priced automobile and whirs about. Probably the only reason why he does not use an airplane is because his congregations refuse to have him risk his life by becoming a "sky pilot," literally as well as figuratively.

The number of strictly up-to-date circuit riders will be greatly increased as a result of the Nationwide Campaign of the Episcopal Church. In the surveys of the needs of the various parishes and dioceses returned to the general headquarters of the Nation-Wide Campaign at 184 East 28 Street, New York City, many requests have been included asking for aid in buying motorcycles and automobiles that the effectiveness of the rector in the sparsely populated sections of the country may be increased many times.

The Right Rev. Hugh L. Burleson of Sioux Falls, SD, Episcopal Bishop of South Dakota, in including the item of automobiles in the survey for that diocese says: "A priest with a machine can do just four times the work out there as a priest without one."

The Right Rev. Clinton L. Quin, Bishop Coadjutor of **Texas**, with headquarters in **Houston**, asks for automobiles for the clergymen in his diocese as does Archdeacon Garner of **Amarillo** for the Diocese of North Texas. There, the territory in charge of each clergyman is large and the distances he has to cover so great that it is deemed indispensable that he be supplied with motor transport.

The Right Rev. James Wise, Bishop of Kansas, wants motorcycles instead of automobiles for a number of his clergy. With them, he will be able to supply a preacher for a number of small towns within sixty miles of **Topeka** every Sunday.

The Rev. Frank Hale Touret, Bishop of Western **Colorado**, also asks for automobiles while the **Right Rev. Paul Matthews of the Diocese of New Jersey wants, in addition to motor cars, a motor truck large enough to transport a priest with all the accessories needed for holding any kind of a religious service—communion, funeral, morning prayer, or wedding—so that out of the way communities in southern New Jersey may enjoy the religious advantages of more populous communities.**

As a result of the Nationwide Campaign, which is to raise both money and workers for the expansion of all Episcopal activities, the dealers in automobiles, motorcycles, and gasoline will find a new customer for their wares and one whose trade is entirely likely to keep on expanding as the vestries learn how much modern means of transportation, add to the amount of work which their rectors can accomplish.

(News Dispatch, Union, NY., January 1, 1920)

Rev. S. E. Carr of Walton traveled more than ninety miles to preach to congregations in Northfield, North Franklin, and East Branch on a recent Sunday, by means of the auto. Old-time circuit riders had nothing on this expounder of the Gospel in the matter of covering distance to carry the message.

(Rural Times., September 14, 1921, Page 1, Image 1)

WILL HAVE MOTOR CAR

Reno County Circuit Rider Has Purchased Machine

Hutchinson, KS, Feb. 16—Reno County believes it has the first motor car circuit rider in **Kansas**. The Rev. W. B. Stevens of the Hutchinson Methodist Episcopal Church Circuit, who preaches at **Mitchell** and **Poplar** country churches, bought a touring car today in which to visit his churches and make pastoral calls.

(The Topeka State Journal., February 16, 1910, LAST EDITION, Page 2, Image 2)

THE MODERN CIRCUIT RIDER

The old type of circuit rider in a new guise is coming back. He will return to do church duty in the **Spokane** country, but will not be known as "circuit rider." He will be known as "convention pastor," and **in place of the saddle horse of his old-time model, will use the passenger coaches or perchance, will be chauffeur of his own automobile**. The plan is being inaugurated by Dr. A. H. Bailey, superintendent of Baptist missions, says the *Spokane Chronicle*; and the duty of the "convention pastor" will be to assist weak churches and look after neglected and undeveloped fields.

(The Monett Times., August 03, 1917, WEEKLY EDITION, Image 12)

GOSPEL CARRIED BY AUTOMOBILE

The family doctor has told in detail the benefits he has derived from the automobile by keeping in closer touch with his practice; the merchant has reported wonderful improvement in the efficiency of his delivery system since the motor car came into vogue; and countless members of other professions and trades have paid glowing tributes to the efficiency of this method of transportation, of labor saved and money made. Now come representatives of the clergy who tell of a work for good, in the interest of the church, accomplished by the automobile.

The old circuit rider, so familiar in thrilling stories of fiction and fact, has given way to the modern country preacher who drives his own car. Whereas the circuit rider formerly spent most of his nights and a greater part of his days in tedious driving from one church to another, the up-to-date rural minister covers twice the territory and accomplishes much greater results without the grueling hardships which were a part of the life of his predecessor. No longer does the average priest or preacher shudder at the thought of an eighteen-mile drive through the country to the home of a sick parishioner. Instead of devoting four or five hours, at least, to a dreary and too often perilous ride across the country, he climbs into his automobile and half an hour later, he is at the home of his friend.

At a recent church gathering, it was stated that the automobile had been one of the church's most paying investments, especially in the rural districts. It is customary for the clergyman or priest in charge of the small, country church to accept other small churches in nearby territory. A single church in a community so small could not support him financially, while three or four churches could furnish him a most comfortable living. The advent of the automobile has made it possible to increase that territory on a remarkable scale. In one village, where the pastor had struggled along to support a family of four on $550 a year, a wealthy farmer made him a present of a machine and arranged to have placed under his charge three more churches in neighboring villages. Each church pays its share of the automobile upkeep. The result is that the pastor now has a salary income of approximately $1,600 a year, an automobile for pleasure, as well as business, and his family is receiving a comfortable living.

It is certain that the automobile is no more popular with any class of people than it is with the church going circles. Its economy in upkeep and efficiency for country driving in all kinds of weather and over every class of road, appear to be the chief factors in making it desirable for that work.

DENVER POST
**(The Ogden Standard., September 02, 1916, 4 P.M. CITY EDITION,
Page 10, Image 10)**

CHAPTER 5

WOMEN CIRCUIT RIDERS

One little-known fact is that there were also women circuit riders. The first one on record was a woman by the name of Helenor Alter Davisson[1] (1823-1876). In 1866, in Indiana, she became the first ordained female deacon in the Methodist tradition; and she traveled with her father, who was also a circuit rider.

Portrait of Helenor M. Davisson, courtesy of Archives and History[2] (edited from original)

A WOMAN CIRCUIT RIDER

Miss Alva Button Is Commissioned as An Itinerate Preacher

Brazil, IN, Sept. 30—To the Lower Wabash Annual Conference of United Brethren in Christ, whose thirty-second session closed the other day, belongs the honor of giving to the church its first lady circuit rider in Miss Alva Button of Greenup, IL. The act authorizing the innovation was passed by the session of the general conference held last May. Only a few days ago, Miss Ella Mishwanger, a graduate of the theological seminary, Dayton, OH, was ordained as an elder at the session of the Central Illinois Conference, being the first woman ordained. At the same conference, Mrs. Elliot was also admitted. Later, Mrs. Bell, wife of an itinerant preacher, was admitted to conference. None of these were assigned to fields of labor.

Miss Button is a young lady of more than average attainments, common sense, and pluck; and it may be said that she possesses beauty, being tall and prepossessing in appearance. She is a native of Chicago; *she* learned to set type in the office of an Illinois newspaper when seventeen years old and afterward became a successful schoolteacher.

When her call to the ministry came, she was a member of the Methodist Episcopal Church, but joined the United Brethren, owing to the similarity of their doctrine and in order to secure admission to conference.

The Westfield Illinois Circuit, to which she was appointed, is one of the first in the conference. It has five appointments, somewhat scattering, but she will preach at the appointments every two weeks. Bishop Kephart and the conference generally give her a cordial welcome, and a bright future is predicted for her.

"She may do all right," said one of the older preachers, "until it comes to immersing some big six-footer in a creek; then she will be left."

"Not a bit of it," said a bystander. "There will not be a man in the crowd but what will throw off his coat and volunteer to do the dunking for her."

(The Manning Times., October 09, 1889, Image 6)

WOMAN CIRCUIT RIDER USES AN AUTOMOBILE

Directs Big Camp Meeting Which Will Open Here Tomorrow

Mrs. Aimee McPherson, twenty-seven years old, modern circuit rider, who has spread the Gospel of her religion from coast to coast as she traveled by automobile, tightened the ropes of the last tent erected at Thirty-fourth Street and Midvale Avenue today and announced everything was in readiness for a big camp meeting.

With Mrs. McPherson as preacher, manager and chief inspiration, the pentecostal revival, under the auspices of the fifteen Pentecostal assemblies of this city, will open tomorrow morning Two hundred living tents have been erected on the grounds in addition to four dormitory tents and the enormous tabernacle.

It is estimated there will be tent room for 500 persons. Many more than that from all sections of the United States and Canada are expected to attend the meetings. Though under the auspices of the pentecostal assemblies, the meetings will be nonsectarian; and the public is invited.

Interest centers about Mrs. McPherson herself. She began preaching ten years ago, when she was just seventeen years old She later married and has two children. She has conducted meetings in all parts of this country and in Canada, where she was born.

She travels in a well-equipped automobile, which contains all the paraphernalia for cooking and sleeping. She is her own manager and has even helped to erect the tents of the meeting here. She is also an editor, publishing monthly a magazine known as the *Bridal Call* and various pamphlets of her own writing.

Beginning Sunday, there will be three meetings a day. In the tabernacle, Mrs. McPherson will speak each evening, and others of her party will conduct the other meetings.

(Evening Public Ledger., July 20, 1918, Night Extra, Page 9, Image 9)

GOD IS STILL USING WOMEN IN THIS HOUR

Acts, 2:17 says, "And it shall come to pass in the last days," saith God, "I will pour out of my Spirit upon all flesh: and your sons and your daughters shall prophesy, and your young men shall see visions, and your old men shall dream dreams:"

Church, Are we not living in the last days?

There are many well-meaning people today who believe that a woman can't share the Gospel with or teach a man. God will use whoever He wants to, to reach as many people as possible. He does not want half of His people to be silenced when there are thousands upon thousands of people who are lost and on their way to hell, and who are in desperate need of a Savior. It is a tactic of the enemy of our souls to silence women.

It is the will of God that ALL should come to repentance. We know that not all will, but we should be about our Father's business working in the harvest fields.

Many women have been allowed to go off to distant, remote, and dangerous lands to preach the Gospel, yet in their home churches, they are told to be silent. This ought not be so!

QUOTES BY FAMOUS FATHERS OF THE FAITH REGARDING WOMEN

John Wesley (1703-1791) was the first Methodist to license women to preach. In his famous sermon, "On Visiting the Sick," he attacked the idea that women be required to be submissive and said of the idea that "women are only to be seen but not heard," that it was "the deepest unkindness . . . and I know not how any women of sense and spirit can submit to it."[3]

"No doubt, holy women of faith were reproached for His name's sake and were accounted to be mad women; but they had a faith which enabled them at that time to overcome the world, and by which they climbed up to heaven."—**George Whitefield (1714-1770)**

"I wish we had a few more women like the woman of Samaria, willing to confess what the Lord Jesus Christ had done for their souls."—D. L. Moody (1837-1899)

CHAPTER 6

PETER CARTWRIGHT: LEGENDARY CIRCUIT RIDER

Many years ago, before the great division occurred between the northern and southern Methodists, there was a well-known preacher in the southwest named Peter Cartwright. Peter did not put on any frills. He went among the mountaineers and wherever duty called him, wearing the homely garb of the frontier, his chief article of attire being a hunting shirt and a girdle. He spoke from the heart, and he reached the hearts of those to whom he spoke. Wherever Peter Cartwright went, the people turned out to hear him, because they felt that they would get the Gospel message from one whose simple, forcible words they could readily grasp. The time came for a conference at Nashville, and Peter Cartwright, with his hunting shirt, was among the attendant preachers. Henry P. Bascom, afterwards bishop, presided and was in personal appearance at least quite a contrast to Peter. Brother Bascom wore a white shirt and was gotten up generally in the style of the clergyman accustomed to the environment of the growing community, already at that time the civic center of Tennessee. Bascom did not approve *of* the get-up of Brother Peter and showed his disappointment by omitting to ask Peter to deliver an address in the church, as was customary in rotation during the conference.

While Peter was not a favorite with Bascom, he was liked by nearly everybody else; and the fame of his rude, effective eloquence had got abroad among Methodists generally, and they wanted to hear him. The pressure on Bascom was so great the he was unable to resist, but he sought to make it as uncomfortable as he could for Peter and Peter's admirers. So, one evening at the close of the daily session, Brother Bascom announced: "Brother Peter Cartwright will deliver a sermon in this church at 6 o'clock tomorrow morning and all who wish to hear him are requested to be present."

The members of the conference and others present were astounded. Peter arose, calmly and deliberately. "Brethren," he said, "I hope everyone of you will be present to hear me. God's message can be spoken just as well at 6 o'clock in the morning as at any other hour, and I will do my best to deliver it."

Peter Cartwright outdid himself in the fervor, the earnestness, and the apostolic spirit that breathed in his every utterance. It was the most effective sermon of the conference, and ministers and laity alike were inspired by it. When Peter had concluded, he was told that General Jackson wished to speak to him. With a hearty grasp of the hand, the General spoke of the impression that the sermon had made on him, at the same time handing Peter $30 to help in his ministry. And thus ended Bascom's foolish attempt to belittle Peter Cartwright.

(Forest City Press., April 06, 1911, Image 3)

PETER CARTWRIGHT

A remarkable character was Peter Cartwright. He was a great, anti-slavery man and struck right and left *at* all who opposed him. One day, on approaching a ferry across the River Illinois, he heard the ferryman swearing terribly at the sermons of Peter Cartwright and threatening that if ever he had to ferry the preacher across, and knew him, he would drown him in the river. Peter, unrecognized, said to the ferryman: "Stranger, I want you to put me across."

"Wait till I'm ready," said the ferryman, and pursued his conversation and strictures upon Peter Cartwright. Having finished, he turned to Peter and said: "Now I'll put you across."

On reaching the middle of the stream, Peter threw his horse's bridle over a stake in the boat and told the ferryman to let go of his pole. "What for?" asked the ferryman.

"Well, you've just been using my name improper like; and said if ever I came this way you would drown me. Now you've got a chance."

"Is your name Peter Cartwright?" asked the ferryman.

"My name is Peter Cartwright."

Instantly, the ferryman seized the preacher; but he did not know Peter's strength; for Peter instantly seized the ferryman, one hand on the nap of his trousers, and plunged him into the water, saying: "I baptize the (splash) in the name of the devil, whose child thou art." Then lifting him up, added: "Did you ever pray?"

"No."

"Then it's time you did."

"Nor never will," answered the ferryman. Splash! Splash! and the ferryman is in the depths again.

"Will you pray?" asked Peter.

The gasping victim shouted: "I'll do anything you bid me."

"Then follow me; 'Our Father which art in Heaven, (etc.)' "

Having acted as clerk, repeating after Peter, the ferryman cried: "Now let me go."

"Not yet," said Peter, "you must make three promises: First that you will repeat that prayer morning and evening as long as you live: secondly, that you will hear every pioneer preacher that comes within five miles of this ferry: and thirdly, that you will put every Methodist preacher over free of expense. Do you promise and vow?"

"I promise," said the ferryman.

And strange to say, that man afterwards became a shining light.

(Bradford Reporter., March 14, 1861, Image 1)

A FORGOTTEN
ANTE-BELLUM CELEBRITY

Peter Cartwright, the Belligerent Frontier Preacher, and His Remarkable Career

By Captain Henry A. Castle, Auditor for the Post Office Department

A LONG AND STRENUOUS CAREER

His ministerial life, after taking orders covered period of more than 65 years, 20 of which were for the most part, given within the limits of the Southern States, he in the meantime being domiciled in Kentucky. He spent 45 years in Illinois, during all of which period he made Pleasant Plains, in Sangamon County, where he owned a farm, his family residence. Fifteen years of his ministry he did duty as a circuit rider in parishes or "circuits," which involved hundreds of miles of itineration, the rude cabins of the frontier being his places for preaching. The remaining 50 years of his clerical life were given to the duties of Presiding Elder, a post to which he was first appointed in 1812, and thereafter, with almost unbroken succession was repeatedly appointed by the Bishops until, in that important office, second only to the Bishopric, he rounded out a half century of efficient supervisory service. In all, he baptized 12,000 persons and preached 15,000 sermons.

Much of the country was without roads—in some instances even devoid of trails—the lonely itinerant having to gauge his course by general direction, across trackless wastes, by certain fixed objects on constantly expanding horizons until his destination was reached in some isolated cabin. The heat of the summer's sun and the more inhospitable rigors of the winter's blasts, unbridged, swollen, and turbulent streams seem never to have impeded his progress, since it is said of him that he seldom missed an appointment. Coming at intervals into these lonely frontier homes with such uniform punctuality must indeed have made his visitations seem to their occupants like those of an evangel. And why not? He was their highway commissioner, their newspaper, their railroad, their telegraph and telephone; he was indeed the voice of one crying in the wilderness, "Prepare ye the way and make the path straight," for a dispensation of which he was the prophet and which he lived to see fulfillment.

His earliest appointments were in circuits embracing areas along the line between Kentucky and Tennessee, extending into both states, and then perhaps the next year far away in the "Ohio country," around Chillicothe. He was allowed by church rules, $80 a year salary. But the country was new, the people were poor, money was almost unknown among them, and during neither of the first years of his arduous traveling service in the ministry, did he receive one-half, even, of the meager allowance. But this fact did not seem to distress the ardent young zealot—he went right on with his work and overcame all its hindrances.

(The National Tribune., June 04, 1903, Page 2, Image 2)

PETER CARTWRIGHT
THE BACKWOODS PREACHER

(From the National Magazine for August)

We once gave a sketch of Peter Cartwright in these pages. It would be unpardonable to omit the adventure of such a character from this class of "jottings;" we must then call him again into your presence, "courteous reader," even if we should repeat some of his stories already told.

He appears broken with years and labors, and you perceive some paralytic tremblings in his attitude and voice; but there is nevertheless a general aspect of strenuous vigor about him. **He looks as if he might yet wrestle with bears and come off conqueror, as we learn he really has heretofore. He is war-worn and weather-beaten. His complexion is bilious, the integuments of his face wrinkled and tough, his eyes small and twinkling, and defended by a heavy pair of spectacles with green side glasses, his mouth compact and full of force, his head large and round, his forehead deeply indented, and his hair—there is no description of that; it looks as if he had poked it into the bag of the Kilkenny cate, and had not had time to comb it since its extrication.** And yet do not suppose there is any ??? caput. Nay, verily; a face more firmly characterized with good nature and gallant generosity is not to be seen. Should we attempt an intellectual portrait of Peter Cartwright, we should summarily say that he is characterized by good sense and good humor. We know not that we can better describe him. He strikes right at the object before him and never fails to hit it; and he has that characteristic of the highest wisdom—brevity, sententiousness. We never knew him to speak in General Conference more than five minutes at once. His humor is always spontaneous—always ready. It sometimes cuts sharply, but is usually genial and generous, relieving rather than exasperating the case. Humor is a rare excellence, but it is not, like gems, valuable chiefly for its rareness; it is intrinsically valuable. It should not be too severely grinned at, with elongated faces, in even ecclesiastical bodies; it often gleams like exhilarating sunlight among lowering clouds of discord, and sometimes dispels them, and does infinitely more than the strongest logic or the loudest rhetoric to remove obstructions to business. Still, a man of combined good sense and good humor is liable to suffer some disparagement. Our poor human nature has a sort of self-complimenting propensity to speak of a superior man with qualifying "but," the import of which is, that though he excels us in some things, we can see in him defects we have not ourselves. He has imagination, "but" he has not much sense; he has humor, "but" he has not much logic. Much of this kind of twaddle is sheer fudge, and something worse. Peter Cartwright is not merely a man of humor but of genuine sagacity; woe be to the man that attempts to circumvent him in debate. If some of his short sayings were divested of their humor and spoken by a *great* man, they would pass for unique utterances of wisdom: as they are, they pass for pertinent jokes—happy bits. Peter Cartwright is a "Doctor of Divinity." Good old George Pickering, when asked once if the Methodists had any Doctors of Divinity, replied, "No, Sir, we don't need them; our divinity has not yet become sick."

Those healthful days seem, however, to have passed, if we may judge from the ample provisions made for theological medication among us nowadays. Some college in the west deemed Peter Cartwright too knowing in the Materia Medica, or too skillful with the scalpel, to die untitled, and, therefore, dubbed him D.D. We know not that he pretends to encyclopedic erudition, or is more skillful than some other doctors we are acquainted with in the learned languages—a knowledge of which is usually presupposed in giving that title; the only learned quotation we ever heard from him was in respect to a matter of business, which seemed to be beyond the reach of his brethren; it was, said he, "*in noampus non-com-atibus*." The learned doctors around him smiled very cognisantly, as they usually do at college commencements when a Latin phrase is quoted which, though unintelligible to the vulgar throng, is always remarkably striking to them.

His fellow soldier in the west, James B. Finley, gives the following further account of him, of which we gave an extract once, but now give it fully:

"Immense was the gathering at the Methodist camp-ground near Springfield, on the second Sunday of September 1832. A powerful magnet had attracted this great mass of people from their homes in many counties, a hundred miles around. The new Presiding Elder, a late arrival from Kentucky, an orator of widespread and wonderful renown, it was known, would thunder on that day. The prestige of his fame had lightened before him, and hence the universal eagerness to hear one concerning whom rumor's trumpet-tongue discoursed so loudly. Morning broke in the azure east, bright and beautiful as a dream of Heaven; but the ex-prodigy had not made his advent. Eleven o'clock came—the regular hour of the detonation of the heavy gun of orthodoxy—and still there was no news of the clerical lion. A common circuit preacher took his place, and sensible of the popular disappointment, increased it by mouthing a miserable failure. The vexed and restless crowd began to disperse, when an event happened to excite afresh their curiosity and concentrate them again denser than ever. A messenger rushed to the pulpit in hot haste and presented a note, which was immediately read out to prevent the people from scattering. The following is a literal copy of that singular epistle:

"Dear Brethren:

The devil has foundered my horse, which will detain me from reaching your tabernacle till evening. I might have performed the journey on foot; but I could not leave poor Paul, especially as he has never left Peter. Horses have no souls to save, and therefore, it is all the more the duty of Christians to take care of their bodies. Watch and pray, and don't let the devil get among you on the sly before candle-light meeting, when I shall be at my post.

Your brother,

PETER CARTWRIGHT

"At length, the day closed. The purple curtain of night fell over the earth from the darkening sky. God's golden fire flashed out in Heaven, and men below kindled their watchfires. The encampment, a village of showy tents, was illuminated with a brilliancy that caused every leaf to shine and sparkle as if all the trees were burnished with a phosphorescent flame. It was a theatre in the open air, on the green award, beneath the starry blue, incomparably more picturesque and gorgeous than any stage scenery, prepared within walls of brick or marble, where the *elite* of cities throng to feast their eyes on beauty and their ears on music.

"Presently a form arose in the pulpit, and commenced giving out a hymn, preliminary to the main exercises, and every eye became riveted to the person of the stranger. Indeed, as someone said of Burke, a single flash of the gazer's vision was enough to reveal the extraordinary man, although, in the present case, it must, for the sake of truth, be acknowledged that the first impression was ambiguous, if not enigmatical and disagreeable. His figure was tall, burly, massive, and seemed even more gigantic than the reality from the crowning foliage of luxuriant, coal-black hair, wreathed into long, curling ringlets. Add a head that looked as large as a half bushel; beetling brows, rough and craggy as fragmentary granite, irradiated at the base by eyes of dark fire; small and twinkling like diamonds in a sea—they were diamonds of the soul, shining in a measureless sea of humor —a swarthy complexion, as if embrowned by a southern sun; rich, rosy lips, always slightly parted, as wearing a perpetual smile; and you have a life-like portrait of the far-famed backwoods preacher.

"Though I heard it all, from the text to the amen, I am forced to despair of any attempt to convey an accurate idea of either the substance or manner of the sermon which followed. There are different sorts of sermons—the argumentary, the dogmatic, the postulary, the persuasive, the punitive, the combative, 'in orthodox blows and knocks,' the logical, and the poetic; but this specimen belonged to none of these categories. It was *sui generis*, and of a news species.

"He began with a loud and beautifully modulated tone, in a voice that rolled on the serene night air like successive peals of thunder. Methodist ministers are celebrated for sonorous voices; but this was matchless in sweetness as well as in power. For the first ten minutes his remarks, being preparatory, were commonplace and uninteresting; but then, all of a sudden, his face reddened, his eyes brightened, his gestures grew animated as the waftures of a torch, and his whole countenance changed into an expression of inimitable humor; and now his wild, waggish, peculiar eloquence poured forth like a mountain torrent. Glancing arrows, with shafts of ridicule, *bon mots*, puns, and side-splitting anecdotes, sparkled, flashed, and flew like hail till the vast auditory was convulsed with laughter. For a while, the more ascetic strove to resist the current of their own spontaneous emotions. These, however, soon discovered that they had undertaken an impossible achievement in thinking to withstand his ???. His every sentence was like a warm finger, tickling the ribs of the hearer. His very looks incited to mirth far more than other people's jokes so that the effort to maintain one's equilibrium only increased the disposition to burst into loud explosions, as every schoolboy has verified in similar cases. At length, the encampment was in a roar, the sternest features relaxed into smiles, and the coldest eyes melted into tears of irrepressible merriment. This continued thirty minutes, while the orator painted the folly of the sinner, which was his theme. I looked on and laughed with the rest, but finally began to fear the result as to the speaker.

" 'How,' I exclaimed, mentally, 'will he ever be able to extricate his audience from that deep whirlpool of humor? If he ends thus, when the merry mood subsides and calm reflection supervenes, will not the revulsion of feeling be deadly to his fame? Will not every hearer realize that he has been trifled in matters of sacred and eternal interests? At all events, there is no prospect of a revival tonight; for even though the orator were a magician, he could not change his subject now and stem the torrent of head-long laughter.'

"But the shaft of my inference fell short of the mark; and even then he commenced to change, not all at once, but gradually, as the wind of a thundercloud. His features lost their comical tinge of pleasantry; his voice grew first earnest, and then solemn, and soon wailed out in the tones of deepest pathos; his eyes were shorn of their mild light, and yielded streams of tears, as the fountain of the hill yielded streams of water. The effect was indescribable, and the rebound of feeling beyond all conception.—He descanted on the horrors of hell, till every shuddering face was turned downward, as if expecting to see the solid globe rent asunder, and the fathomless, fiery gulf yawn from beneath. Brave men moaned; and fair, fashionable women, covered with silken drapery and *belighted* with gems, shrieked as if a knife were working among their heartstrings.

"Again he changed the theme—sketched the joys of a righteous death—its faith, its hope, its winged raptures, and angels attending the spirit to it starry home—with such force, great and evident belief, that all eyes were turned toward Heaven; and the entire congregation started to their feet, as if to hail the vision of angels at which the finger of the preacher seemed to be pointed, elevated as it was on high to the full length of his arm.

"He then made a call for mourners *to come* to the altar, and five hundred, many of them till that night infidels, rushed forward and prostrated themselves on their knees. The meetings continued for more than two weeks, and more than a thousand converts were added to the Church. From that time, his success was unparalleled, and the fact is chiefly due to his inimitable wit and masterly eloquence that Methodism is now the prevailing religion in Illinois.

"He was distinguished by one very unclerical peculiarity—combativeness. His battles, although always apparently in the defensive, were as numerous as the celebrated Bowie. The only difference was this, that Bowie fought with deadly weapons, while the itinerant used but his enormous fist, which was effective, however, in the speedy settlement of belligerent issues as any knife or pistol ever forged cut of steel. Let the reader judge from the following anecdote:

"At the Camp Meeting held at Alton in the Autumn of 1833, the worshippers were annoyed by a set of desperadoes from St. Louis, under the control of Mike Fink, a notorious bully, the triumphant hero of countless fights, in none of which he ever met an equal or even second. The coarse, drunken ruffians carried it with a high hand, outraged the men and insulted the women, so as to threaten the dissolution of all pious exercises; and yet such was the terror the name of their leader, Fink, inspired, that no one could be found brave enough to face his prowess.

"At last, one day, when Cartwright ascended the pulpit to hold forth, the desperadoes, on the outskirts of the encampment, raised a yell so deafening as to drown utterly every other sound. The preacher's dark eyes shot lightning. He deposited his Bible, drew off his coat, and remarked aloud:

" 'Wait for a few minutes, My Brethren, while I go and make the devil pray.'

"He then proceeded with a smile on his lips to the focus of the tumult, and addressed the chief bully—

" 'Mr. Fink, I have come to make you pray.'

"The desperado rubbed back the tangled festoons of his blood-red hair, arched his huge brows with a comical expression, and replied:

" 'By golly, I'd like to see you do it, old snorter.'

" 'very well,' said Mr. Cartwright; 'will these gentlemen, your courteous friends, agree not to show foul play!'

" 'In course they will. They're rale grit, and won't do nothin' but the clear thing, so they won't,' rejoined Fink, indignantly.

" 'Are you ready?' asked the preacher.

" 'Ready as a race-hoss with a light rider,' answered Fink, squaring his ponderous person for the combat.

"The bully spoke too soon; for scarcely had the words left his lips when Cartwright made a prodigious bound toward his antagonist, and accompanied it with a quick, shooting punch of his herculean fist, which fell, crushing the other's chin, and hurried him to the earth like lead. Then, even his intoxicated comrades, filled with involuntary admiration at the feat, gave a cheer. But Fink was up in a moment, and rushed upon his enemy, exclaiming,

" 'That warn't done fair, *no* it warn't.'

"He aimed a ferocious stroke, which the preacher parried with his left band, and, grasping his throat with his right, crushed him down as if he had been an infant. Fink struggled, squirmed, and writhed in the dust; but all to no purpose; for the strong, muscular fingers held his windpipe as in the jaws of an iron vice. When he began to turn purple in the face and ceased to resist, Mr. Cartwright slackened his hold and inquired, 'Will you pray now?'

" 'I doesn't know a word how,' gasped Fink.

" 'Repeat after me.'

"'Well, if I must, I must,' answered Fink; 'because you're the devil himself.'

"The preacher then said the Lord's Prayer line by line, and the conquered bully responded in the same way, when the victor permitted him to rise.

"At the consummation, the rowdies roared three boisterous cheers, and Fink shook Cartwright by the hand, declaring:

" 'By golly, you're some beans in a barfight. I'd rather set to with an old "he" bar dog-days. You can pass this 'ere crowd of nose-smashers, blast your pictur'l.'

"Afterward, Fink's party behaved with extreme decorum, and the preacher resumed his Bible and pulpit."

An odd scene that certainly *was*, and "not very apostolic," say you, sober reader. We join you in the remark, but it is character, as we said in another case.

We give it as a fact from our old friend Finley—a fact that illustrates not only the character of the man, but of the country and its early times. "Circumstances alter cases," is a popular proverb in the West, as well as elsewhere; and even good men are heard, occasionally, to affirm out there, that Lynch law is better than no law.

Mr. Bungay, in his volume of "Offhand Takings of Noticeable Man of our Age," says that he heard Peter, at Boston, during the last General Conference of the Methodist Episcopal Church, and thus describes the occasion:

"The great Western preacher has arrived and is now searching the well-thumbed Bible for his text. Quite a number of distinguished divines are present. The preacher looks like a backwoodsman, whose face has been bronzed at the plough. His black hair, straggling seven ways for Sunday, is slightly tinged with the frost of age. A strip of black silk is twisted around his neck, and a shirt collar, scrupulously clean, is turned down over it. He is of ordinary size, dresses plainly, and looks like a man perfectly free from affliction. In a faltering voice, be reads hymns. The choir read the words to sweet and solemn music— a fervent prayer goes up on the wings of faith—another hymn is read and sung—the 19th verse of the 11th chapter of Matthew is selected for his text. Now, the old pioneer preacher, who has waded swamps, forded rivers, threaded forests, travelled with Indians, fought with bears and wolves, preached in the woods, and slept in the field or on the prairie at night, is standing before us. Look at him, ye gentlemen with white neckcloths and black coats, who ride in carriages over smooth roads to supply churches with cushioned pews and soft benches to kneel on. How would you like to labor for nothing among wild beasts and board yourselves in a climate where the ague shakes the settlers over the grave two-thirds of the year? Would you exchange your fat livings, and fine palaces, and unread libraries, for black bread and dry venison, a log hut, and the society of bears and blue racers? God bless the brave, wise, and good men to whom we are so much indebted for the blessings we enjoy. He says he would make an apology if he thought it would enable him to preach better, for he is afflicted with a severe cold. 'Some folks,' said he, 'say I am fifty years behind the age. 'God knows' he continued, 'I am willing to be a thousand behind such an age. Religion is always of age, and can talk or run without stilts or silver slippers.' He concluded an able and interesting discourse, which elicited undivided attention, with the following fact: 'During a splendid revival of religion at the West, a young preacher, manufactured in one of your theological shops out here, came to lend a helping hand. I knew he could not handle Methodist's tools without cutting his fingers, but he was very officious. Well, we had a gale—a pentecostal gale—and sinners fell without looking for a soft place, and Christians fought the devil on their knees. Well, this little man would tell those who were groaning under the conviction to be composed. I stood this as long as I could and finally sent him to speak with a great, stout, athletic man, who was bellowing like a bull in a net, while I tried to undo the mischief he had done to others. He told this powerful man to be composed, but I told him to pray like thunder—just at that instant, the grace of God shone in upon his soul, and he was so delirious with delight; he seized the little man in his hands, holding him up, bounded like a buck through the congregation.' It is impossible for the pen to do justice to this fact. The speaker moved us all to tears and smiles at the same moment, while he said what few men would venture to say."

While he was preaching, years ago, Gen. Jackson entered the Church, when a Pastor seated in the pulpit gave his "brother Cartwright" a nudge and whispered that the old hero had just come in—as much as to advise, "Now be particular in what you say." But Peter, to the astonishment of everyone, louder than ever, exclaimed, "Who cares for General Jackson? He'll go to hell as soon as anybody, if he doesn't repent!"

When the sermon—a homemade one—was ended, a friend asked the General what he thought of that rough, old fellow and received the answer, "Sir, give me twenty thousand such men, and I'll whip the world, including the devil!"

It is quite possible, Brother Reader, that yours and our notions might not quite agree with the General's; yet neither of us can fail to see in this eccentric but veteran evangelist, the man of his times and his circumstances. And you, Dear Sir, starched, and brushed, and perfumed, who now recline in the stuffed armchair of your garnished study, wondering why the world should take any interest in such a specimen of humanity—what kind of specimen would you have been? What would you have done in the rough battles through which this weatherworn, but jolly-hearted old man has borne brawny but ever-??? God bless the old man, with all his oddities; and may he fight his way into Heaven.

Peter Cartwright joined the "Old Western Conference" in 1805, though he began to travel a year earlier, we believe. He was a young man—only about eighteen years old—when he entered the itinerant field, and he has been in its foremost struggles ever since. The "Old Western Conference" was in that day the only one beyond the Alleghanies. It extended from Detroit to Natchez, and each of its Districts comprised a Territory about equal to two of the present Conferences beyond the mountains. Those were the days of great moral battles in that vast field; and the men who fought them were made great, some of them gigantically so, by their circumstances. Among them were Young, Walker, Shinn, M'Kendree, Burke, Lakin, Blackman, and Quinn, and similar mighty men. Cartwright began his regular travels with Lakin on Salt River Circuit (save the name!) Most of his fellow heroes have gone to their rest; but they gained the field and fortified their cause all over it. The few remnants of the old corps should be cherished and honored by their Church.

(Eastern State Journal., August 24, 1855, Page 1, Image 1)

CHAPTER 7

CIRCUIT RIDERS MEMORIALIZED

In 1924, two statues of circuit riders were erected—one in Salem, Oregon, at the state capitol and the other in Washington, DC (of Francis Asbury). They were erected to honor circuit riders who have gone before us in the United States.

Listed below are parts of the program from the dedication of the monument in Salem, Oregon.

THE CIRCUIT RIDER[1]
(*Official Ceremony Program*)

THE CHRISTIAN MINISTER & THE STATE
By the Rev. Bishop William O. Shepard, D.D., LL.D.

...On June 3, in the capital of the nation, there is to be unveiled an equestrian statue of Francis Asbury, the prince of Circuit Riders, and here in the capital of the farthest state is unveiled a like statue to commemorative of the numberless Circuit Riders who have been heralds of patriotism and Christianity across the land. ...Jason Lee, David Leslie, Gustavus and H. K. Hines, John McKinney, John F. DeVore, Father Wilbur, Robert Booth, and T. L. Jones are the men to be crowned today by filial and grateful hands. Their names should be repeated over and over, that the thousands who enjoy the benefits they secured may know their benefactors.

THE AMERICAN PIONEER
By Joseph N. Teal

...It is said that in 1832, a council was held by the chiefs of the Flat Head Indians to consider a story they had heard of a white man's God. It may have been from an occasional trapper that they first heard the story, but the interest was aroused, and they wanted to learn the truth. As St. Louis was then the chief trading point for the hunter and trapper, to that city four Indians were sent to get the details of this strange tale. Tradition and history tell they learned but little. Two of them died in St. Louis. The other two, disappointed and disheartened, turned toward the land of their fathers, no wiser than when they left their wigwams in the far West. One died on the way—the other may have reached home. Here ends this part of the story—but it was not the end. It was but the beginning. The story was published in the newspapers, and it came to the notice of those whose life was devoted to the service of God.

The missionary spirit was fanned into flame at the thought of vast numbers of human beings living and dying without the knowledge of the Gospel and all that it means, and with the unquenchable ardor and zeal of the crusader, the pioneer missionaries, the men who blazed the way for others, soon were struggling forward, fighting their way across ranges, fording or swimming dangerous streams, enduring all things to answer the call of the Indians for knowledge of the white man's God.

The Circuit Rider was a natural product of the time in which he lived. The population was small and scattered over wide areas. There were no means of locomotion except the horse and going about on foot. The roads, such as they were, were few, always rough, and frequently impassable. Trails led here and there, from settlement to settlement, from cabin to cabin, through the wilderness. At first there were no churches, and even when their building began, they were very few and far apart. To reach and serve the scattered people, it was necessary to carry the Gospel to them. In sickness and in health, in hours of sadness and of happiness, The Circuit Rider was oftentimes the only comforter, the only one on whom to lean, the only connection between the tenant of the cabin and the outside world. He left no call unanswered. He was always at the command of those who needed him. The missionary of God was not only the herald of the Gospel but, in words of another, "He was architect, carpenter, ox driver, axman, painter, blacksmith, and pastor." While preaching the Word, he was not only earning a living for himself and his family but was aiding others in the most practical of ways.

And it must not be understood that these early missionaries were uneducated, uncouth, or uncultured men. How much they knew of the sciences, I know not, but of the Word of God they knew much. However, their daily labors left them scant time for study. Accordingly, not infrequently—as depicted in this group—the Circuit Rider would read his Bible and collect his thoughts while riding slowly to a meeting place where people were assembled to hear his message. There were no cowards, physical, spiritual, or intellectual, among them. Nor was there place for weaklings in those days. Fearless, faithful, and direct, they went about preaching the Bible and what it taught, doing good, helping this one, encouraging that one, facing hardships of every kind. They suffered patiently, they endured much. **Some suffered even martyrdom by the hand of the Indian wielding the murderous tomahawk. Others in treading the treacherous rapids of the rivers and mountain streams were swept away. Indeed, death and danger faced them on every hand. Like the great Apostle to the Gentiles (*Paul*), he could not ineptly say: "In journeyings often, in perils of waters, in perils of robbers... in perils by the heathen... in perils in the wilderness, in perils in the sea... in weariness and painfulness, in watchings often, in hunger and thirst, in fastings often, in** cold and nakedness." So also, as with Paul, it was literally true of this itinerant outrider for the Kingdom of God—"I die daily."

In many instances, devoted women shared with these missionaries every danger, every hardship, every trial. What a glorious roll do the names of the early missionaries make!

Then, when the growth of the population seemed to justify the effort, they directed their energies to laying the foundations of educational and charitable institutions which continue to this day, ever exerting a powerful influence in molding the character of men and women of the Northwest. The Willamette University at Salem is one of these institutions.

When one contemplates the wonderful country, its resources, both actual and potential, and what we now refer to as its early days, it is difficult to avoid dealing somewhat with its history and the part The Circuit Rider played within. There were indeed giants in those days. While this magnificent memorial is representative of a type, one may be pardoned, in considering the progress made in the last 100 years, for referring to a few facts.

…The Circuit Rider is a particularly fond memory to the pioneers. It is but natural that this should be so. And we are now gathered together to join in dedicating this magnificent and lifelike memorial to his life and character. It is peculiarly fitting that the state owes this splendid gift to the patriotism and generosity of Robert A. Booth, a pioneer and the son of a pioneer Circuit Rider. It is a great pleasure, a great satisfaction, for me to have the opportunity of joining in this unveiling, and I appreciate the great compliment paid me in asking me to speak on this occasion. No words can add anything to the standing and character as a citizen and as a man of one I am honored in calling my friend, Robert A. Booth. His life is a part of the history and growth of his native state and his example an inspiration to all who know him or have come within the influence of his life. His desire is to perpetuate the memory of all the early missionaries of whatever race or creed. While this memorial was inspired by the love and reverence Mr. Booth bore his father, it is not intended to commemorate any individual, but is erected in honor of all who honored the greatest call that can come to a man. Notwithstanding this desire of Mr. Booth, there are occasions, there are times, where history and the future require facts to be stated. In this instance, I feel certain everyone at once will concede the propriety. It makes this occasion doubly interesting for all to know that the father of Mr. Booth was a pioneer Circuit Rider, one of the type I have tried to depict, and that Mr. Booth is a native of Oregon, having been born in Yamhill country in May 1858, which in itself makes him a pioneer. His father was a true type of the pioneer missionary, a type fast disappearing. His name was Robert Booth. He was born in England in 1820; came to America with his parents in 1830; lived in a and about New York six years and then went by steamer to New Orleans, up the Mississippi to St. Louis, and thence crossed the plains to Oregon by ox team with his wife and four children in 1852. He joined the Oregon Conference of the Methodist Episcopal Church in 1855 and remained a member until his death, July 1917, at the age of 97 years. His last charge was Grants Pass. To paraphrase concerning the woman in Proverbs, "Let his own work praise him in the gates."

In closing, **I wish that I could leave with you the picture of The Circuit Rider as I see him. He was not materialist nor opportunist. Abraham like, "He looked for a city that hath foundations, whose builder and maker is God." His faith was founded on verities and was anchored deep in the Word of God. In honoring him, we honor ourselves, and in contemplating his life and work, we are elevated to a higher plane.** He had the vision of a prophet, but with it all, he had to deal with the problems of everyday life. His life was passed in a country in the making, with but few of the instrumentalities of civilized life to aid him. Obstacles that might well have caused him to falter were treated as but trifles light as air in the path he was following. Dangers and death he faced calmly as part of his life. Doing all the things that fell to the lot of the early missionary, baptizing the babies, ministering to the sick, marrying the youths, burying the dead, preaching and exhorting and helping in every way—is it a matter for surprise that these brave and simple, God-fearing souls should have endeared themselves to their friends and neighbors and now that they are gone, have left their memory a priceless heritage. Such men as these do not die. With the passing of time and the separation of the dross from the gold, their lives and their examples stand our more and more radiantly as beacon lights to guide others on their way. They will live forever in the hearts of those they leave behind.

CHAPTER 8

EVANGELISM

THE HEARTBEAT OF GOD

THE GREAT COMMISSION

*And Jesus came and spake unto them, saying, "**All power is given unto me in heaven and in earth.***

*"**Go ye therefore, and teach all nations, baptizing them in the name of the Father, and of the Son, and of the Holy Ghost:***

*"**Teaching them to observe all things whatsoever I have commanded you: and, lo, I am with you always, even unto the end of the world. Amen.***" Matthew 28:18-20 (KJV)

*"The Lord is not slack concerning his promise (*of His return*), as some men count slackness; but (*He*) is longsuffering to us-ward, **not willing that any should perish, but that ALL should come to repentance**."* 2 Peter 3:9

God wants everyone to be in Heaven with Him when they leave this planet. There is not a single person who He wants to see go to hell. We were created in His likeness to be in fellowship with Him for all of eternity!

Evangelize ... Evangelize ... Evangelize!

The circuit riders made great sacrifices in order to share the Good News of the Gospel with people who sometimes had never even heard it before. They were doing their part, to the best of their ability, by partnering with God in EVANGELISM.

We can share the Good News with people as well. It may not look the same as it did when the circuit riders were testifying, but we can be a light by sharing our own stories with people and, if appropriate, offering to pray with them. We can sow seeds wherever we go. Sharing doesn't have to be difficult or weird. We can simply ask God to lead, guide, and direct us as we talk with others about what Jesus has done in our own lives. Paul's actions were a good example of this.

Therefore he (Paul) *reasoned in the synagogue with the Jews and with the Gentile worshipers, and **in the marketplace daily** with those who happened to be there.* Acts 17:17 (NKJV)

Why not take a step of faith and talk to somebody about Jesus today? Be bold and courageous!

KEYS TO EFFECTIVELY REACHING PEOPLE

God never changes, but the way that He interacts with people at different times in history sometimes does. Even when Jesus was on the planet, He didn't follow a pattern, He did things differently in different situations. That is why it is so important to **be SPIRIT-LED believers**.

God goes before us and prepares the way in the spirit realm for what He's calling us to do in the temporal realm.

The Bible says that Jesus did nothing apart from the will of the Father. In other words, He was listening and then doing. He was our perfect example. This is why we need to become good listeners and be sensitive to what He is saying and how He is leading so that we can be in alignment with what He wants to do right now.

*For as many as are **led by the Spirit of God**, they are the sons of God.* Romans 8:14 (KJV)

*"**My sheep hear My voice**, and I know them, and they follow Me."* John 10:27 (NKJV)

We can all learn to recognize the voice of God, but we have too many people out there who are making decisions based on feelings, head knowledge, or outward signs; but not nearly enough who are being led by the Holy Spirit. As we learn to recognize His voice through His Word and other ways that He reveals Himself to us, we will become more and more effective at sharing the Gospel.

We also need to **operate in the POWER of the Holy Spirit!**

*"**But ye shall receive POWER**, after that the **Holy Ghost** is come upon you: and **ye shall be witnesses unto me both in Jerusalem, and in all Judaea, and in Samaria, and unto the uttermost part of the earth**."* Acts 1:8 (KJV)

Jesus said that the main reason that He was sending His Spirit was for us to be powerful witnesses, to BOLDLY testify of Him wherever we are—whether we are at home, in our communities, in another part of the country, or someplace else in the world.

We also need to be careful that we are the same person during the week (at our home, jobs, in the store, etc.)

as the one we bring to church with us on Sunday mornings. The way that we live our lives is important. People are watching us. **Every time that we walk out of the door of our homes, we're entering the mission field.** Let's be mindful that people see the way that we treat others; and our attitudes, words, and actions can impact them in both positive and negative ways. Let's be people whose lives are a good witness!

It is also very important that we don't neglect the poor and oppressed. God put this in His Word repeatedly for a reason. It is very easy to have a temporal mindset and place value on people based on their social standing or economic status. God doesn't see things the same way. He places equal value on all people.

When the people of God were fasting and Heaven was silent, God gave them this message:

"Is this not the fast that I have chosen:
To loose the bonds of wickedness,
To undo the heavy burdens,
To let the oppressed go free,
And that you break every yoke?
Is it not to share your bread with the hungry,
And that you bring to your house the poor who are cast out;
When you see the naked, that you cover him,
And not hide yourself from your own flesh?
Then your light shall break forth like the morning,
Your healing shall spring forth speedily,
And your righteousness shall go before you;
The glory of the LORD shall be your rear guard.
Then you shall call, and the LORD will answer;
You shall cry, and He will say, 'Here I am.'" Isaiah 58:6-9 (KJV)

When Paul and Barnabas were being sent off to minister to the Gentiles, this is what they were told: *All they asked was* *that we should continue to **remember the poor**, the very thing I had been eager to do all along.* Galatians 2:10 (NKJV)

*Pure religion and undefiled before God and the Father is this, **to visit the fatherless*** (orphans) ***and widows*** *in their affliction,* James 1:27 (KJV)

In helping the poor, we often have opportunities to pray for people and share the Gospel. We can miss "God Moments" when we turn a blind eye to those among us who are needy.

God cares about everyone, and He wants all to come into a right relationship with Him. We are blessed to have opportunities to partner with Him in bringing about His desire for people, everywhere we go. It is an honor and a privilege!

CHAPTER 9

YOU ARE CALLED

The Word of the Lord to the prophet, Jeremiah: *"Before I formed you in the womb, I knew you; Before you were born, I sanctified you; I ordained you a prophet to the nations."* Jeremiah 1:5 (NKJV)

*"For I know the thoughts that I think toward you, saith the LORD, thoughts of peace, and not of evil, **to give you an expected end**."* Jeremiah 29:11 (KJV)

God had a plan for Jeremiah's life before He even formed him in the womb. He had a plan for the disciples' lives, the circuit riders' lives, and He has a plan for your life as well.

Consider the circuit riders' determination and perseverance to fulfill God's plans and purposes for their lives. They had sheer determination and zeal that carried them through the hardships that they had to endure; like exposure to the elements (extreme heat and freezing temperatures); threats from wild animals; and sometimes lack of adequate food, clothing, and/or shelter.

Be encouraged, My Friend, God created you with special plans and purpose for your life as well! Just like He did with the circuit riders, God wants to use you, too.

"WHAT IS MY PURPOSE OR MY CALL?"

It is partially your position in your family, but it goes far beyond that. Each one of us was born with a call on our lives, to make a difference for eternity. People don't realize just how important their calls are.

If you don't already know what yours is, you need to seek God about this. He wants to reveal your call to you, fill you with His Spirit, and empower you to walk in it. He created you for relationship with Him and to walk in your calling!

If our forefathers hadn't walked in their callings, God would have given their God-given purposes to others. He will find a way for His will to be accomplished on Earth; however, He may need to do it differently than His first plan, because we have free will. The choice is ours, whether or not to walk in our call. He won't force us.

Each of our lives is intertwined with many other people. We all have a circle of influence. If we look at every day as an opportunity to partner with God, then we will realize that He wants to use us to make a difference for His Kingdom.

Remember that God often used people who didn't measure up to the standards of the "religious" people of the time in which they were living in. He specializes in using those who don't think they measure up to the world's standards.

*For you see your calling, brethren, that **not many wise according to the flesh, not many mighty, not many noble, are called**. But God has chosen the foolish things of the world to put to shame the wise, and God has chosen the weak things of the world to put to shame the things which are mighty; and the base things of the world and the things which are despised God has chosen, and the things which are not, to bring to nothing the things that are, that no flesh should glory in His presence. But of Him you are in Christ Jesus, who became for us wisdom from God—and righteousness and sanctification and redemption—that, as it is written, "He who glories, let him glory in the LORD."* 1 Corinthians 1:26-31 (NKJV)

I love this quote by Smith Wigglesworth because it sums up how God operates:

**"God does not call those who are equipped;
He equips those whom He has called."**

**WALK IN YOUR CALLING
AND FULFILL YOUR CALL!**

.

CHAPTER 10

HELPFUL SCRIPTURES TO MEMORIZE ON EVANGELISM

THE GREAT COMMISION

And Jesus came and spoke to them, saying, "All authority has been given to Me in heaven and on earth. Go therefore and make disciples of all the nations, baptizing them in the name of the Father and of the Son and of the Holy Spirit, teaching them to observe all things that I have commanded you; and lo, I am with you always, even to the end of the age." Amen. Matthew 28:18-20 (NKJV)

And He (Jesus*) said to them, "Go into all the world and preach the Gospel to every creature. He who believes and is baptized will be saved; but he who does not believe will be condemned. And these signs will follow those who believe: In My name they will cast out demons; they will speak with new tongues; they will take up serpents; and if they drink anything deadly, it will by no means hurt them; they will lay hands on the sick, and they will recover."* Mark 16:16-18 (NKJV)

The Great Commission was given to the disciples, but it wasn't only given for them. It was given to you and me as well. God wants us all to go into all the world and preach the Good News of the Gospel of Jesus Christ.

GOD WANTS EVERYONE TO BE SAVED

The Lord is not slack concerning His promise, *as some count slackness, but is longsuffering toward us,* ***not willing that any should perish but that all should come to repentance****.* 2 Peter 3:9 (NKJV)

For this is good and acceptable in the sight of God ***our Savior, who desires all men to be saved and to come to the knowledge of the truth.*** 1 Timothy 2:3-4 (NKJV)

God's Word is clear that He wants everyone to be saved—even the person who we may think is beyond His reach. Make no mistake about it, He wants everyone to be with Him for all of eternity. On the cross, He paid the price for every single individual who would ever live, whether they would eventually receive Him as Lord and Savior or not, even the ones who will not end up in Heaven someday. That is LOVE like no other! Nothing is too difficult for Him!

THE HARVEST FIELDS ARE RIPE

*Then He (*Jesus*) said to them, "****The harvest truly is great, but the laborers are few; therefore*** *pray the Lord of the harvest to send out laborers into His harvest."* Luke 10:2 (NKJV)

Are you willing to be one of these laborers who Jesus was referring to? Are you willing to go wherever He sends you? Do you want to be a part of the great end-time harvest of souls on the planet today? God may simply call you to speak to your next-door neighbor, or He may call you to go to another country. It is our responsibility to be willing to PRAY and GO, wherever He sends us.

In Closing

I pray that this book has challenged you about the seriousness of your commitment level to God. The examples of the circuit riders' lives really put things in perspective about what matters for eternity. Remember that God wants to use YOU for Kingdom purposes … FOR A SUCH A TIME AS THIS.

May God bless you, prepare you, strengthen you, lead you, guide you, give you wisdom, and use you to help bring in the final harvest of souls in these last days in which we're living.

SALVATION PRAYER

If you don't already know Jesus as your Lord and Savior and you want to, please pray the following prayer from your heart to enter into a relationship with Him:

Dear Jesus,

I admit that I'm a sinner, and I need You. Thank you for dying on the cross in my place and taking my punishment. Please forgive me for my sins, and come into my heart and be my Savior and my Lord. Please help me to live for You from this day forward. Thank you for making me part of Your family. In Jesus' Name, Amen.

If you prayed this prayer sincerely from your heart, you are now a child of God. You have just taken your first step in your journey with Him. Welcome to His family!

BIBLIOGRAPHY

Chapter 1: Typical Life of a Circuit Rider

1. Holy, "Knock-'Em-Down" Preachers, John H. Wagner, https://christianhistoryinstitute.org/magazine/article/knock-em-down-preachers/, Accessed Date: January 9, 2020, Used with permission January 21, 2020 [Christian History originally published this article in Christian History Issue #45 in 1995]

Chapter 2: Circuit Rider Trivia and Tidbits

1. Holy, "Knock-'Em-Down" Preachers, John H. Wagner, https://christianhistoryinstitute.org/magazine/article/knock-em-down-preachers/, Accessed Date: January 9, 2020, Used with permission January 21, 2020 [Christian History originally published this article in Christian History Issue #45 in 1995]

Chapter 5: Women Circuit Riders

1. Timeline of Women in Ministry (February 22, 2019), Copyright © 2019 United Methodist Communications, https://www.umc.org/en/content/timeline-of-women-in-methodism, Accessed Date: January 9, 2020, Used with permission January 17, 2020.

2. "When Did the Church First Ordain Women?" "Ask the UMC" Copyright © 2018 United Methodist Communications. https://www.umc.org/en/content/ask-the-umc-when-did-the-church-first-ordain-women, Accessed Date: January 9, 2020, Used with permission January 17, 2020.

3. "Helenor Alter Davisson, Circuit Rider and Minister–Historical Notes" "Susan Ozmore" https://wingateumc.wordpress.com/2015/08/03/helenor-alter-davisson-circuit-rider-and-minister/ Accessed Date: January 9, 2020, Used with permission January 21, 2020. ["Historical

Notes" "Susan Ozmore," First published in our monthly church newsletter, "*The Wingate Messenger*."]

Chapter 7: Circuit Riders Memorialized

1. Proceedings at the Unveiling and Dedication of The Circuit Rider, State Capital Grounds, Salem, Oregon, Saturday, April 19, 1924; Accessed Date: 2/7/2020, Used with permission 2/6/2020 from http://www.roaroregon.org/documents/circuit-rider-dedication.pdf

Made in the USA
Middletown, DE
10 May 2022